God's Cure for Antagonism in the Church

Jesus Christ in Word and Sacrament Ministry

God's Cure For Antagonism In The Church:
Jesus Christ in Word and Sacrament Ministry

Copyright © 2016 John F. Wurst
4791 N. Reynolds Road – Lake Ann, Michigan 49650
1-231-944-9553

All rights reserved. No part of this publication may be reproduced, stored in a retrieval system, or transmitted, in any form or by any means, electronic, mechanical, photocopying, recording, or otherwise, without the prior written permission of John F. Wurst.

Cover Photo Copyright © Andrii Ospishchev/Shutterstock.com
War Chapter Photo Copyright © Bill Frische / Shutterstock.com
Unity Chapter Photo Copyright © Zvonimir Atletic / Shutterstock.com
Love Chapter Photo Copyright © TheModernCanvas / Shutterstock.com
Mercy Chapter Photo Copyright © Nicku / Shutterstock.com
Witness Chapter Photo © photolike / Shutterstock.com
Forgiveness Chapter Photo © Oleg Golovnev / Shutterstock.com

Scripture taken from the New King James Version®. Copyright © 1982 by Thomas Nelson. Used by permission. All rights reserved.

Quotations from the Lutheran Confessions are from Concordia: The Lutheran Confessions, second edition; edited by Paul McCain, et al., Copyright © 2006 Concordia Publishing House. All rights reserved.

Quotations with the abbreviation LSB are from Lutheran Service Book, Copyright © 2006 Concordia Publishing House. All rights reserved.

Quotations from the Small Catechism are from Luther's Small Catechism, Copyright © 2006 Concordia Publishing House. All rights reserved.

ISBN-13: 978-1535446570

To my beloved bride Tamara

Contents

ACKNOWLEDGMENTS 9

PREFACE 11

INTRODUCTION 13

WAR 17

UNITY 23
- You – the sinner 26
- You – the Baptized 27
- You and the Church catholic 29
- You and the congregation 35

LOVE 41
- God's love for mankind 43
- God's love for the world through the Christ 45
- God's love shared through faith in the Christ 48

MERCY 51
- Mercy – Christ rescued you from the darkness 54
- Mercy – Christ's absolution for you 55
- Mercy – Christ's teaching to sustain the faith He created in you 57
- Mercy – Christ's giving of His Body and Blood to you for the forgiveness of your sins 59
- Mercy – The sharing of Christ's mercy 61
- with others 61

WITNESS 67
- LEGAL ACCOUNTS 70
- CONFESSIONAL ACCOUNTS 71
  - *Confession of sins* 74
  - *Confession of faith* 75
  - *Confession of praise* 76
- BLOOD ACCOUNTS 80

FORGIVENESS 83

ENDNOTES 116

Acknowledgments

I give thanks to the God and Father of my Lord Jesus Christ every day I breathe. I thank Him for His love, His forgiveness, His grace and mercy which never end, and for the everlasting life His Son gave to me in His resurrection from the dead.

I am thankful to my seminary professors who taught and prepared me for the Holy Ministry. I especially want to thank Professor John Pless who prepared me to minister to the sick and dying. To Dr. Gieschen for his love of the Gospel of John and the Greek language. To, then professor, Chad Bird for his love of Hebrew and for teaching me the beautiful language. I also thank Chad for opening my eyes to the Gospel of Jesus in the Old Testament, especially the Book of Genesis. And finally, to Dr. Naomichi Masaki for taking me into the depths of God's grace in His sacraments, especially the Lord's Supper. Thank you all for your mentoring.

I am thankful for the Rev. James Strawn and his instruction during the summer of my 2006 mini-Vicarage at Saint James Lutheran Church in Archbold, Ohio. I learned much from Pastor Strawn that summer and I will never forget him or the lessons he gave me.

I am thankful for the Dr. Daniel May, President of the Indiana District and Professor Richard Nuffer (Emeritus) for not giving up on me when my initial Vicarage assignment was cancelled.

I am thankful for the members of Saint John + Bingen Lutheran Church in Decatur, Indiana for having me as their Vicar during my last year of seminary. I thank my supervisor, Rev. Daniel Dahling, and my brother in Christ, Dr. Daniel Brege, for their instruction and guidance during my Vicarage.

I want to thank two pastors for their counsel during my ministry in Minnesota. These two servants of Christ prayed for me, my family, and my congregation throughout the entire time of suffering and healing. I give thanks to my Lord Jesus for His faithful servants, the Reverend David Schoessow, Pastor at Christ Lutheran Church in Superior, Wisconsin and the Reverend Robert Wurst Jr., Pastor at St. Paul Lutheran Church in Cedar, Michigan. Brothers, thank you for your wisdom, counsel, prayers, and friendship.

This book would not be written if it weren't for the love and faithfulness of my members at Lutheran Church of Christ the King in Duluth, Minnesota. I thank God every day for these fine people. They provided much care for me and my wife when I was their pastor. They came to visit when I was sick and recovering from surgery. They stood by me through the dark days until the darkest day came, when the congregation closed on Sunday, August 18, 2013.

Finally, I want to thank my family. They stood by me and my wife through it all. However, there is no greater warrior than my beloved wife and helper whom the Lord gave me.

I am so thankful for Tami and her love and faithfulness. She provided much encouragement to me. She supported me when I was in despair. She prayed for me every day. She loved me when I was a grouch. She took care of me when I was sick. Through it all, she remained calm, bearing my burden which was unknown to her. I love her for all this and so much more. Thank you, Tami.

Preface

During my time of study at Concordia Theological Seminary in Fort Wayne, Indiana (2003-2008), one of my Pastoral Ministry and Missions classes required the reading of a book titled, *Antagonists in the Church: How to Identify and Deal with Destructive Conflict* by Kenneth C. Haugk.

I remember thinking about the future and saying to myself, this could never happen in the church, maybe in the business world, but never in the church. I remember thinking that the church is a holy place; a place of refuge and prayer; a place where people go to worship God; give thanks for the blessings in their lives, and receive the forgiveness of their sins. However, I found antagonism in a holy place very uncharacteristic. As I reflect on my seminary days, I realize how ignorant I was.

In this work, I will describe what I call the war that divided the congregation. This section is not what this book is about, rather, it sets the tone for the cure God delivered to His little flock in the aftermath of the war.

This book is written to show the approach that I took with the congregation after the dissension ended on December 24 ✠ A.D. 2010. I am indebted to Rev. Matthew C. Harrison, President of The Lutheran Church--Missouri Synod for his foresight in developing a theme for the Synod called, Witness, Mercy, Life Together.

I used this theme to commence the healing process with the Lutheran Christians I was called to serve at The Lutheran Church of Christ the King.

May the God and Father of our Lord Jesus Christ have mercy upon me where I have erred in any way. I give thanks to God for healing the congregation and give Him all the glory.

Introduction

This book is about who Christians are in Jesus Christ. This book follows a young pastor and the approach taken to bring healing to the congregation he served in the Evangelical Lutheran Church.

After suffering from two years of dissension, antagonism, and excessive and blatant passive aggressive behavior, the Lord of the Church delivered the young pastor and the congregation. He delivered them through the teaching of the Word. He delivered them in answer to their prayers for mercy and grace. He delivered them through His means of grace; the Word and the Lord's Supper.

This book is about the work of God in a small inner-city congregation in the Northland of Minnesota. This book is about how Jesus, God's only-begotten Son, unites Christians in His Name. It is about His love for Christians and the mercy He extends to them in their lives. This book is about bearing witness, which is, testifying to the world about Jesus as the Savior of the world. It is about forgiveness; God's forgiveness for the sinner, and also the sinners forgiving one another.

I am the young pastor. I cannot express to you how much God's Word strengthened me during my ministry from August 2008-2013. I know in my heart that communication is vital to people who interact together on a day-to-day basis. Without communication, everyone just walks around avoiding one another fearing they will upset one another.

Without communication, people harbor ill will in their hearts toward their neighbors, their pastor, their life-long friends, and so on. Hatred builds up until one day because no one will talk to anybody, the whole community erupts and explodes; the antagonists revealed. Those who dissent come out of the darkness and the passive aggressive people prey on the weak.

Then it seems that the next logical step is to devise a special method of taking care of the situation that took 40-50 years to create because of a lack of teaching and communicating. Yes, that's it. We'll use a special program called "reconciliation." We'll begin talking with an outsider in the room.

Reconciliation is not about some "special program" devised by man. When St. Paul says, "Now all things are of God, who has reconciled us to Himself through Jesus Christ, and has given us the ministry of reconciliation," (2 Cor. 5:18) then there is no need for man-made programs. The Church needs God's Word. She needs to exercise the Office of the Keys. The Office of the Keys is the ministry of reconciliation.

St. Paul is talking about the holy ministry of Word and Sacrament. He is talking about confession and absolution. Our Lord Jesus gave us His instructions on how to handle antagonism and dissension in the Church. Our Lord taught us in His Word how to deal with a brother who hates us.

This book is about submerging the life of the hurting Christian, whether pastor or layman, into the Word of God, where He alone gives His immortal medicine to those who suffer.

This book teaches about the life Christians received in Holy Baptism. It shows in the first section how the Christian is brought into the body of Christ in Holy Baptism and sustained through God's means of grace throughout life.

This book is primarily about the love God has for the world through His Son Jesus. It teaches us that God's love is ours to share with one another, and how love covers a multitude of sins.

This book concludes with the greatest gift that Jesus gave to His Church, namely, the Office of the Keys, that is, the forgiving and binding of sins. When innocent people get caught up in the hatred and power struggles of others, they get hurt. They want answers. They want to know everything is going to be alright. They want to know that God loves them. They want to know that their pastor loves them. They just need someone to listen to them, hold them, and tell them that it's going to be alright.

There is no special program that I, as a young pastor, know of that can do this for the suffering and weak Christian. So, I turned to the only place I know. I turned to God's Word. There, I mined the gems of God's Holy Writ and discovered what to tell my flock. I discovered the words to say to bring them peace. I unveiled the beauty of the cross where Jesus died to tell them that everything is going to be alright.

I hope you enjoy this little book.

May the grace of our Lord Jesus Christ the love of God and the communion of the Holy Spirit be with you. Amen.

Rev. John F. Wurst
All Saints Day
01 November ✠ A.D. 2016

WAR

Destroy the pastor at all costs!

Jesus said, "Behold, I send you out as sheep in the midst of wolves. Therefore be wise as serpents and harmless as doves." – Matthew 10:16

WAR

The date is August 11, 2008. I was installed as the pastor of the congregation just the day before. I come into my study, at the church, to unpack my library.

When I arrive, there is a man waiting for me. I introduce myself and invite him in. I asked him what I could do for him. He replied, with tears welling up in his eyes, "I want a transfer for my family." I asked him why and what happened. He didn't want to talk about. He simply stated that another member told him to leave and not come back. He was very distraught. I offered to pray with him. He declined. I prayed for him after he left my study.

I found my chair. Sat down. I thought to myself, what is the devil doing in this place? Where is Christ? I had some reading to do in the Bible.

The purpose of this book is healing. It is to show how God Cures Antagonism in the Church through His Son, Jesus Christ with His Word and Sacraments. Let me touch on a couple of the other major events that set this war in motion.

I believe the main ignitor of the war occurred around Christmas 2008. During the Advent season, I preached on the Great O Antiphons each Sunday and Wednesday for four weeks. I only selected two Scriptures lessons for each service. So, to eliminate a lot of movement, I asked the five liturgical assistants to sit with their families during Advent. I would do the reading of Scripture.

Around the middle of December or so, one of the men asked me about scheduling the liturgical assistants for January. I informed him to leave them off. I would continue to do the reading of Scripture. He concurred. My mistake was I forgot to mention this plan of action to the five men who were serving as liturgical assistants.

When they received their schedules, they were a little bit confused and upset that they lost one of their duties. We met informally in the hall way. I asked them one question. Has God given this task to you to do? You can use the Scriptures and Lutheran Confessions to answer the question.

The following week, the men came to me with their answers. Three of them said, No. God has not given it to them. He gave it to you pastor. The fourth man went further with his answer and said that they were reading the Scriptures out of necessity when the congregation was without a pastor. They just continued the practice. Now, he said, you're here so we don't have that necessity any more.

The fifth man of the group was not very understanding. He opposed my decision to eliminate the liturgical assistants from reading the Scriptures. He could find no just cause for my request. In fact, after the other four men departed, he indicated his temperament by crossing his arms across his chest. He stopped vocalizing his thoughts and ideas. His countenance fell dramatically. I knew he was upset.

To make a long story short, I made the decision. I told him the others found the resolution. I was sorry he did not. He stood against the Word of God on the duties of the pastor versus the duties of the lay person.

Another major issue in 2009 was the cancellation of the children's Christmas program. As Christmas was fast approaching, I inquired of the status of the children's Christmas program. I was told the committee got a little behind. One day, I went into the church where the children were practicing. I asked to see the materials.

I quickly deduced that the material was not doctrinally sound. I asked if there was a backup program. There was not. I had to cancel the children's Christmas program for doctrinal reasons.

Of course, there was a certain level of disappointment and sadness. It is difficult for the children to understand these things. However, one of the grandmothers got upset with me. She asked me why. I told her. She asked, Can't you just let them do the program anyway and fix this problem next year? I said no. The problem is now. I had to fix it immediately.

Anyway, this member was upset with me for a long time. Eventually, she transferred to another congregation.

The last big event that took place was, I believe, in 2010. I discovered that many members were meeting privately at one of their homes to discuss getting rid of me, their pastor. For the lack of a better word, I had a rebellion on my hands.

The members were upset. They were meeting in secret. They had plans and charges against me. I was not ordering anyone to do anything. I did uphold and defend the Word of God against false teaching and sinful actions. Rebellion is dissent. Dissent is disobedience. Dissent is disapproval. I say, come and talk to me about it.

Basically, no one wanted to come and talk. In fact, one member, the same man mentioned earlier concerning the liturgical assistant duties, wrote to the District President without talking to me first. *(The District President is an elected official who oversees a geographical area of pastors and congregations.)*

In June 2010, this man wanted to meet and talk. He asked for several people to be in attendance. The meeting got underway with prayer. I asked the first question of him, Why are we here? I wanted to hear what was on his mind for the past two years.

He sat there, with his wife at his side, and said nothing for the entire time of the meeting.

This was the last of the major events. There were smaller things that surfaced. I attended to them individually. However, at the end of the day, I was not heard. I was not honoured. The people did what they wanted.

On December 24, 2010, all of the dissenters (antagonists) were released from membership of the Lutheran Church of Christ the King. What follows in this book is the process I used to bring healing and understanding to the faithful members who remained.

The congregation eventually closed her doors on Sunday, August 18, 2013.

Lord, have mercy upon us.

UNITY

Christians are united in Christ when they are Baptized in the Name of the Father and + of the Son and of the Holy Spirit.

Baptism of Jesus in the Jordan River

UNITY

God is faithful, by whom you were called into the fellowship of His Son, Jesus Christ our Lord.

1 Corinthians 1:9

What does unity mean? We often think of unity as being one, likeminded; maybe unity is best described as race, religion, or creed.

Are we Christians one because we are Americans? No. Are we one because we are Scandinavians? No. Are we one because we are all Minnesotans living in the Northland? No. Are we one because we're in the same family? No. What, if anything, then causes us to say we are one? What does it mean to be one that is, united together?

We could look for the answers to our questions by looking in all the wrong places. We could search the dictionaries, textbooks, legal documents, and even the Constitution of the United States and we will never find the answers we seek.

There is only one place to find the truth; God's Word alone holds the truth for all mankind. What does God have to say on the matter of Christian unity?

Let's take a look at this question of unity in the body of Christ in the following major sections:

I. **You – the sinner**
II. **You – the Baptized**
III. **You and the Church catholic**
IV. **You and the congregation**

You – the sinner

First, let's take a look at the unity that is yours due to sin. You are among great company. You come from a long line of sinners like Adam, Eve, Noah, David, Jonah, Peter, and St. Paul.

As a sinner, you are part of the greatest and largest community of the world. You are united together with all people past, present, and future because of the Fall of mankind in the Garden of Eden when Adam and Eve disobeyed God and heeded the word of Satan. (Genesis 3)

As a sinner, **original sin** infects you. St. Paul writes, "Therefore, just as sin came into the world through one man, and death through sin, and so death spread to all men because all sinned…" (Romans 5:12) (cf. Ephesians 2:1-3; Psalm 51; Genesis 5:3; John 2:24-25)

St. Paul also talks about our **actual sin** in the New Testament where he writes, "for all have sinned and fall short of the glory of God." (Romans 3:23) Jesus Himself explains this in His discourse on the relationship of believers to Himself. Jesus says, "I am the vine; you are the branches. Whoever abides in me and I in him, bears much fruit, **for without me you can do nothing**." (John 15:5) Apart from Christ, we are lost and doomed to suffer the wrath of the Father and to die in our iniquity. Apart from Christ, we will be separated from the love of God forever. The Psalmists writes, "The wicked shall return to Sheol, all the nations that forget God." (Psalm 9:17) That old saying is true, "There will be a lot of good people in hell."

Now is the time for you to repent of your sins. Repent and believe on the Name of the Eternal Son of God, Jesus the Christ, who died to save you from your sins, death, and the power of the devil. IT'S TIME! REPENT and turn from your wickedness and "seek the Lord while He may be found, call upon Him while He is near." (Isaiah 55:6)

You – the Baptized

Alright, so you don't want to live in hell forever apart from God and His love. St. Luke writes in the Acts of the Apostles, "Now when they heard this they were cut to the heart, and said to Peter and the rest of the apostles, 'Brothers, what shall we do?' And Peter said to them, 'Repent and be baptized every one of you in the name of Jesus Christ for the forgiveness of your sins, and you will receive the gift of the Holy Spirit. For the promise is for you and to your children and to all who are far off, as many as the Lord our God will call.'" (Acts of the Apostles 2:37-39)

The bigger question is this, "How are you able to make such a statement?" Do you know God? Who is He? Where is He? Is He a loving God? You cannot ask or answer any of these questions as a sinner apart from Christ. Don't worry; God revealed Himself to the world in His Son, Jesus the Christ. So now you want to know more about God and His Son – GOOD!

Jesus said, "For God so loved the world that he gave his only begotten Son, that whoever believes in him should not perish but have everlasting life." (John 3:16) God reveals Himself to the world but the world does not comprehend Him. (John 1:5) But you know God. You know Jesus. You know because Christ Himself took you in His arms and Baptized you in the waters of Holy Baptism.

Jesus said to Nicodemus, "Truly, truly, I say to you, unless one is born of water and the Spirit, he cannot enter the kingdom of God. That which is born of the flesh is flesh, and that which is born of the Spirit is spirit." (John 3:5-6) When Jesus Baptized you, you became a partaker of the heavenly kingdom. You are among the saints. You were given life from above.

Titus writes, "But when the goodness and loving kindness of God our Savior appeared, he saved us, not because of works are done by us in righteousness, but according to his mercy, by the washing of regeneration and renewal of the Holy Spirit, whom he poured out on us richly through Jesus Christ our Savior, so that being justified by his grace we might become heirs according to the hope of eternal life. The saying is trustworthy, and I want you to insist on these things so that those who have believed in God may be careful to devote themselves to good works. These things are excellent and profitable for people." (Titus 3:4-8)

You are all sons of God. (Galatians 3:26a) You are one body in Christ. (Ephesians 4:4) It is not your doing nor your righteousness which achieves this bond, rather, it is the Christ working outside of you creating the saving faith within you. It is the Christ who has done all things for you. The Christ continues to serve you daily as He forgives your sins and strengthens your faith. The Christ is the one who feeds you through His Word and Sacrament. He does all this because of His love for you – His Children.

In Holy Baptism, Christ made you a member of His Church. St. Paul writes, "But when the fullness of time had come, God sent forth his Son, born of woman, born under the law, to redeem those who were under the law, so that we might receive adoption as sons. And because you are sons, God has sent the Spirit of his Son into our hearts, crying, "Abba! Father!" So you are no longer a slave, but a son, and if a son, then an heir through God." (Galatians 4:4-7)

The unity or communion (*koinōnía*) we have with one another in Baptism is because "God is faithful, by whom we were called into the fellowship of His Son, Jesus Christ the Lord." (1 Corinthians 1:9)

Our unity is God's work. Our unity is in Christ. The world cannot unify us. We can't unite ourselves. We cannot know true unity by any standard of mankind. Only in Christ are we one body.

Christ unites us by His Blood, which, He shed for us, on our behalf, on the cross. Christ unites us together when He forgives us all our sins. Without the forgiveness of sins, we are alone, lost, and condemned.

We are united in Christ because of His means of grace. We are united in Word and Sacrament. We are united in Christ and called the Baptized sons of God. (Galatians 3:26) We are the priesthood of the Baptized. We are one in Christ, given a life of love and service to one another in Christ. Our mission is to tell others the Good News of salvation that Jesus Christ, the Son of God, died for all men to save all people from sin, death, and the power of the devil.

You and the Church catholic

Through your Baptism, our Lord Jesus the Christ brought you into communion (***koinōnía***) with all the saints and more importantly with Him and His Father who is in heaven. You probably don't remember this most important day, and that's alright. What is important is that you believe Jesus did this for you. He called you and received you unto Himself. (Matthew 18:1-5)

Let's review our relationship, as Christians, to Christ Himself.

The Relationship of Believers to Christ

"I am the true vine, and my Father is the vinedresser. Every branch in me that does not bear fruit he takes away, and every branch that does bear fruit he prunes, that it may bear more fruit. Already you are clean because of the word that I have spoken to you. Abide in me, and I in you. As the branch cannot bear fruit by itself, unless it abides in the vine, neither can you, unless you abide in me. I am the vine; you are the branches. Whoever abides in me and I in him, he it is that bears much fruit, for apart from me you can do nothing. If anyone does not abide in me he is thrown away like a branch and withers; and the branches are gathered, thrown into the fire, and burned. If you abide in me, and my words abide in you, ask whatever you wish, and it will be done for you. By this, my Father is glorified, that you bear much fruit and so prove to be my disciples. As the Father has loved me, so have I loved you. Abide in my love. If you keep my commandments, you will abide in my love, just as I have kept my Father's commandments and abide in his love. These things I have spoken to you, that my joy may be in you, and that your joy may be full." (John 15:1-11)

In Holy Baptism, you became a member of the invisible church. You became a member of the one holy catholic church, that is, the one spiritual body of believers (saints), whose head is Christ. (See Romans 12:4-5; Ephesians 4:3-6)

The one holy catholic church is where ever the Gospel of Jesus Christ is preached in its purity, and the holy sacraments administered according to the Gospel. The Gospel of Jesus Christ and the Sacraments are the "marks of the church." (See Isaiah 55:10-11)

This new life you have in Christ is given and sustained by the power of the Holy Spirit. Hear what Jesus says, "It is the Spirit who gives life; the flesh is no help at all. The words that I have spoken to you are spirit and life." (John 6:63)

When we make our confession concerning the Holy Spirit in the Creeds, we confess that the Holy Spirit gives life! The Third Article of the Creed is all about the giving of life!

Now, let's review our relationship to one another, in Christ, as the Baptized (visible Church).

The Relationship of Believers to Each Other

"This is my commandment, that you love one another as I have loved you. Greater love has no one than this that someone lay down his life for his friends. You are my friends if you do what I command you. No longer do I call you servants, for the servant, does not know what his master is doing; but I have called you friends, for all that I have heard from my Father I have made known to you. You did not choose me, but I chose you and appointed you that you should go and bear fruit and that your fruit should abide, so that whatever you ask the Father in my name, he may give it to you. These things I command you so that you will love one another." (John 15:12-17)

We are also one, united in Christ, here at The Lutheran Church of Christ the King in Duluth, Minnesota. However, the church in this place is not your church nor is it mine. The Church belongs to Christ. She is His Bride.

Here in this holy place, Christ is serving His people. He forgives. He baptizes. He teaches. He feeds. He blesses. Yes, this congregation is the visible church here in Duluth. You know this is Christ's Church by what Christ is doing in this place.

The church is not only made up of people but more importantly, it is people gathered around the marks of the church; Word and Sacraments. St. Ignatius said it this way, "Ubi Christus ibi ecclesia" which means, Where CHRIST is there is the CHURCH.

So, where do you find the Church? You find her where the bishop preaches the Word in its truth and purity and where the Sacraments administered according to Christ's institution. There the Word is being preached and taught, and the sacraments administered. The Church confesses Christ in Word and Sacrament. You cannot confess Christ apart from what He is doing in distributing His gifts through preaching and the Lord's Supper.

You know where the Church is by the "marks of the church." There are seven marks to know and remember as Christians.[1] They are:

- ☐ **The Word of God**
- ☐ **The Sacrament of Holy Baptism**
- ☐ **The Sacrament of the Lord's Supper**
- ☐ **The Office of the Keys**
- ☐ **Call and Ordination**
- ☐ **Prayers**
- ☐ **The sacred cross**

We must also remember that the visible church has unbelievers in her midst. There are hypocrites in her midst of which, against which sin, we the Baptized pray that God will guard us.

The unity we have in this congregation is not because of anything we have done, are doing, or ever will do in our lives. Our unity is because of Christ and in Christ.

Finally, let's review our relationship to those around us in our community and world.

The Relationship of Believers to the World

"If the world hates you, know that it has hated me before it hated you. If you were of the world, the world would love you as its own; but because you are not of the world, but I chose you out of the world, therefore the world hates you. Remember the word that I said to you: 'A servant is not greater than his master.' If they persecuted me, they will also persecute you. If they kept my word, they will also keep yours. But all these things they will do to you on account of my name, because they do not know him who sent me. If I had not come and spoken to them, they would not have been guilty of sin, but now they have no excuse for their sin. Whoever hates me hates my Father also. If I had not done among them the works that no one else did, they would not be guilty of sin, but now they have seen and hated both me and my Father. But the word that is written in their Law must be fulfilled: 'They hated me without a cause.'" (John 15:18-25)

In Holy Baptism, you were united with the Bride of Christ, His Church. The next logical question is, what is the Church? You were given life from above through the power of the Holy Spirit.

Our Lord Jesus kept you in communion with Himself and His Bride, the Church, throughout your young life by bringing you to Church and Sunday School. He did this through the power of His Spirit who "calls, gathers, enlightens, and sanctifies the whole Christian Church on earth, and keeps it with Jesus Christ in the one true faith."[2] (SC 147)

So, let's talk more about the communion of saints that you are a part of through the washing and regeneration you underwent by the Holy Spirit in Baptism. What is this communion? Why did you confess to believing in the communion of saints at your Confirmation? Why do you confess this in the Creed each week during the Divine Service?

The communion of saints is another name for the Church catholic, that is, the Church universal. The Church is the communion of saints, that is, the total number of those who believe on the Name of Jesus the Christ. St. Paul writes, "So then you are no longer strangers and aliens, but you are **fellow citizens with the saints and members of the household of God**, built on the foundation of the apostles and prophets, Christ Jesus himself being the cornerstone, in whom the whole structure, **being joined together**, grows into a holy temple in the Lord. In him, you also are being **built together** into a dwelling place for God by the Spirit." (Ephesians 2:19-22)

Jesus also refers to the communion of saints in His discourse on the Good Shepherd in the Gospel according to St. John. Jesus says, "...just as the Father knows me and I know the Father; and I lay down my life for the sheep. And I have other sheep that are not of this fold. I must bring them also, and they will listen to my voice. *So there will be one flock*, one shepherd." (John 10:15-16)

The communion we share with one another is special because of Jesus. He binds us together in His Blood, which, He shed for us on the cross. Our communion together, that is, our Life Together, is the work of God. God is building His Church through the power of the Holy Spirit through the means of grace; Word and Sacraments. We are bound together by the Holy Spirit. Christ works through His means of grace to deliver to you His forgiveness for all your sins. (See 2 Corinthians 5:19) We are sure of these promises of God, through Jesus the Christ, because God keeps His promises in Christ. (See Romans 8:38-39 and 2 Timothy 1:12)

The unity or communion we share together is because God is working to preserve His Church. We believe, teach, and confess this because "There is one body and one Spirit—just as you were called to the one hope that belongs to your call— *one Lord, one faith, one baptism*." (Ephesians 4:4-5)

As sinners given life from above in Holy Baptism, we have vowed, by the grace of God, to hear the Word of God and to receive the Lord's Supper faithfully. We receive the Lord's Supper together because of our common and faithful confession. We believe, teach, and confess that only those of the same confession (*unity/communion*) can partake of the Lord's Supper at the altar. Our confession in this matter is called Close Communion.[3]

At our Confirmation, we also vowed, by the grace of God, to live according to the Word of God, and in faith (*unity/communion*), word, and deed, to remain true to God, Father, Son, and Holy Spirit even unto death. Did you hear your vow? You vowed to live in faith, that is, *unity and communion* with one another in Christ.

And finally, you vowed, by the grace of God, to continue steadfast in this confession (**unity/communion**) and Church (unity) and to suffer all, even death, rather than fall away from it.

So as we reflect on who we are first as sinners, lost and condemned because of our sin, we know, as a matter of fact, we will live because of what Jesus, the eternal Son of God has already done for us in His atoning sacrifice on the cross. We will live, with Christ when He calls us home to glory. We live, today, in Christ, because He saved us in Holy Baptism and wrote the Name of the one true God Father, Son, and Holy Ghost, on our soul and wrote our names in the Book of Life. (Rev. 21:27)

Earlier, I mentioned we are members of the priesthood of the baptized. In Holy Baptism, we became members of the priesthood of all believers. (1 Peter 2:4-10) Christ numbers us among the saints. (Revelation 14:1-5)

As we reflect on our lives as saint and sinners simultaneously (*simul justus et peccator*), we come to the final part of our discussion on unity. We have made the pilgrimage from the womb to adulthood. Now it is time to discuss our lives together in the Church.

You and the congregation

St. Paul teaches, "I therefore, a prisoner for the Lord, urge you to walk in a manner worthy of the calling to which you have been called, with all humility and gentleness, with patience, bearing with one another in love, **eager to maintain the unity** of the Spirit in the bond of peace. There is one body and one Spirit—just as you were called to the one hope that belongs to your call— one Lord, one faith, one baptism, one God and Father of all, who is over all and through all and in all." (Ephesians 4:1-6)

Did you hear St. Paul? He said we are to be eager to maintain the unity (willingness and cooperation). What is he referring? Paul is referring to the faith God gave to all of us in Holy Baptism. Paul is talking about living in Christ. We are truly one because God's Spirit made the Church one in Christ. (LSB note on Eph. 4:3)

Christians are to live in Christ. Is this a strange phenomenon in America and the world in which we live? What does it mean to live in Christ? So we don't lose focus, the prepositional phrase, "in Christ," is a communal statement. To live in Christ defines a lifestyle which is given by God through faith in Jesus Christ.

The Christian life together is a life lived in love. The love we have to give is not ours but Christ's. We love because He first loved us. (1 John 4:19) Our life together is lived through faith. Our life together is a life of confession and absolution. Our confession of unity manifests when we say "I forgive you." There cannot be unity apart from Christ. There cannot be unity apart from the forgiving of sins. Unity results from the forgiveness of sins.

We must all remember that all sin is unbelief. Unbelief is the sure way to everlasting condemnation. However, Christ gives us the gift of repentance and absolution. We use this gift, called the Office of the Keys, to bear one another's burdens (Galatians 6:1-5). If we have loveless thoughts, all we will produce is loveless deeds. Christ commands us to love one another (John 15:12 and Ephesians 4:2)

St. Paul writes, "Blessed be the God and Father of our Lord Jesus Christ, who has blessed us in Christ with every spiritual blessing in the heavenly places, even as he chose us in him before the foundation of the world, that we should be holy and blameless before him. In love, he predestined us for adoption as sons through Jesus Christ, according to the purpose of his will, to the praise of his glorious grace, with which he has blessed us in the Beloved. In him, we have redemption through his blood, the forgiveness of our trespasses, according to the riches of his grace, which he lavished upon us, in all wisdom and insight making known to us the mystery of his will, according to his purpose, which he set forth in Christ as a plan for the fullness of time, **to unite all things in him**, things in heaven and things on earth." (Ephesians 1:3-10)

St. Paul writes to the Church in Corinth describing how they, the Christians and many members of the Church, are one in the Body of Christ. "For just as the body is one and has many members, and all the members of the body, though many, are one body, so it is with Christ. For in one Spirit, we were all baptized into one body—Jews or Greeks, slaves or free—and all were made to drink of one Spirit. For the body does not consist of one member but of many. If the foot should say, "Because I am not a hand, I do not belong to the body," that would not make it any less a part of the body. And if the ear should say, "Because I am not an eye, I do not belong to the body," that would not make it any less a part of the body. If the whole body were an eye, where would be the sense of hearing? If the whole body were an ear, where would be the sense of smell? But as it is, God arranged the members in the body, each one of them, as he chose. If all were a single member, where would the body be? As it is, there are many parts, yet one body. The eye cannot say to the hand, "I have no need of you," nor again the head to the feet, "I have no need of you." On the contrary, the parts of the body that seem to be weaker are indispensable, and on those parts of the body that we think less honorable we bestow the greater honor, and our unpresentable parts are treated with greater modesty, which our more presentable parts do not require. But God has so composed the body, giving greater honor to the part that lacked it, that there may be no division in the body, but that the members may have the same care for one another. If one member suffers, all suffer together; if one member is honored, all rejoice together." (1 Corinthians 12:12-26)

St. Paul writes, "For as in one body we have many members, and the members do not all have the same function, so we, though many, are one body in Christ, and individually members one of another." (Romans 12:4-5) In the context of chapter 12, St. Paul is describing our lives as Christians as a living sacrifice. He describes in detail how God gives each member of the Body of Christ gifts and how each member is to use those gifts.

When we think outside the box, that is, when we start thinking inside the small box of Holy Scripture, God reveals to us the sanctified life in His Son Jesus Christ. When we live out our Baptism and live together in love because of the Christ and His atoning sacrifice on the cross, then we begin to appreciate all that God is doing for us in our lives.

I had a pastor in the LCMS explain it to me this way. Each of us is a member of the Body of Christ. Just as the body has individual members, each with its distinct vocation. If the big toe gets stubbed on the couch, what does the rest of the body do and feel? The rest of the body reacts in pain and suffering. All the members react to bring comfort to the big toe. St. Paul writes to Church in Corinth, "If one member suffers, all the members suffer with it; or if one member honored, all the members rejoice with it." (1 Corinthians 12:26)

Does this story tell of the life of unity here in this holy place? We must discern between friendship (worldly concept) and fellowship (church concept). Man builds friendships. Fellowship in Christ is the work of God.

As we share fellowship with one another in this holy place, living under the cross of Christ, what happens when one of us gets hurt? What happens when one of us is suffering? Do we all get hurt? Do we all suffer? What if one of the members is rejoicing, do we all rejoice? Or, do we all go about our separate lives and do what is good for ourselves without regard for others? Do we have some real close friends that we may let in and rejoice or suffer with us but at the same time ban the rest of the Body of Christ from joining our suffering and rejoicing?

St. Paul tells us, "I appeal to you, brothers, by the name of our Lord Jesus Christ, that all of you agree, and that there be no divisions among you, but that you be united in the same mind and the same judgment." (1 Corinthians 1:10) As Christians, we are not to be divisive but confessing and forgiving.

The unity, communion, life together that we share in Christ is not our own doing. Rather, our life together comes from outside of us. The Reformers expressed it this way: Our righteousness is an "alien righteousness," a righteousness that comes from outside of us (***extra nos***).[4]

We share the "alien righteousness" Christ gives us with one another because of faith. The Apostle James writes, "But someone will say, "You have faith and I have works." Show me your faith apart from your works, and I will show you my faith by my works." (James 2:18)

How can we live together, as Christians, without serving (*diakōnia*) one another through faith in Christ? We can't. REPENT! For the sake of His Son, Jesus, our Father, who is in heaven, will forgive us all our sins. Forgiven, we are restored to the Church, the family, our brothers, and sisters in Christ. When we receive God's forgiveness, we are whole again and united with the Bride of Christ in Christ, our Good Shepherd.

LOVE

Love is more than an emotion. Love is a divine gift shared with others through faith in Jesus Christ.

LOVE

For God so loved the world that He gave His only begotten Son, that whoever believes in Him should not perish but have everlasting life.

John 3:16

The Lord be with you. In the last chapter, I brought you a discussion on Unity. I asked you what unity is? The answer we found that the Holy Scriptures defines unity is in the Christ. As we learned, the eternal Son of God unites us together in Holy Baptism when He claims us to be His own. He binds us together in His Blood when He serves us His Holy Supper for the forgiveness of our sins, life, and salvation.

How did this all happen? How did it happen that the Christ came and entered His creation to redeem us, forgive us, teach us, and give us His promises? All of this happened because of divine love. Let's take a few minutes now and examine the Holy Scriptures to discover this love and how it is ours to share with one another and the world through examination of the following areas.

† **God's love for mankind.**
† **God's love for the world through the Christ.**
† **God's love shared through faith in the Christ.**

The first area we want to examine is:

God's love for mankind.

In the Book of Genesis, Moses teaches us that after the Fall, "...they heard the sound of the LORD God walking in the garden in the cool of the day, and the man and his wife hid themselves from the presence of the LORD God among the trees of the garden. But the LORD God called to the man and said to him, 'Where are you?' And he said, 'I heard the sound of you in the garden, and I was afraid, because I was naked, and I hid myself.'" (Genesis 3:8-10)

Adam and Eve were ashamed because they were naked. They knew that what they had done was bad, really bad. I can only imagine what they were thinking. Maybe it went something like this: The LORD is going to be furious with us. He told us not to eat of the Tree of Knowledge of Good and Evil. What have we done? Oh, we're in trouble now. Do you remember what He said? The LORD said that the day we eat of it, we shall surely die. I don't want to die.

Even though Adam and Eve disobeyed, the LORD doesn't mean the LORD didn't still love them. The LORD gave them His promise that He would save them from their sin. The LORD said, "I will put enmity between you and the woman, and between your offspring and her offspring; he shall bruise your head, and you shall bruise his heel." (Genesis 3:15) The LORD promised Adam, Eve, and the world a Savior. The Son will appease the wrath of His Father and restore communion between the Father and His creatures.

You must remember, that when we, like Adam and Eve, try to fulfill our needs apart from God, our work and effort are always insufficient. Adam and Eve sewed fig leaves together and made themselves loincloths. (Genesis 3:7) Adam and Eve's efforts were minimal at best. However, the LORD sacrificed innocent beasts and provided full coverings for Adam and Eve lest they die from exposure.

"The skins that the LORD covered Adam and Eve are iconic of the Gospel. Here the Lord shows that He will provide what is necessary to hide the shame of His creatures, and that provision comes only by the death of an innocent victim. And the Victim Christ, let it be remembered, is Himself stripped when He is sacrificed, that being naked, He might clothe us with Himself."[5]

Our hope, as was the same for Adam and Eve and all the world, is in the Christ, God's only-begotten Son, who laid His life down in death on the cross to atone for our sins and the sins of the world. Our only hope of salvation is Jesus the Christ, our Lord, and Savior.

St. Paul reminds us, "I therefore, a prisoner for the Lord, urge you to walk in a manner worthy of the calling to which you have been called, with all humility and gentleness, with patience, bearing with one another in love, eager to maintain the unity of the Spirit in the bond of peace. There is one body and one Spirit—just as you were called to the one hope that belongs to your call— one Lord, one faith, one baptism, one God and Father of all, who is over all and through all and in all." (Ephesians 4:1-6)

The second area we want to examine is:

God's love for the world through the Christ.

St. John writes, "For God so loved the world that He gave His only begotten □□Son, that whoever believes in Him should not perish but have everlasting life." (John 3:16) Did you hear what Jesus, the Son of God said? His Father loved the world. Love is why the Father sent His only-begotten Son into the world.

When we ask ourselves because we forget so often, why did the Father send His Son into the world, then we remember how much love God has for us, sinners? As we discussed in the first section, Adam and Eve disobeyed the Lord and sought their glory. They wanted to be like God knowing good and evil.

In their disobedience, Adam and Eve brought sin and death into God's perfect creation. By their disobedience, by ignoring the Word of God, their sin separated them from the love of God. The perfect union they once shared with God was now shattered and gone. They were lost and condemned in their sin.

For this reason, the Lord promised to send His Son to save His people. We say in our liturgy, "Our help is in the Name of the Lord – who made heaven and earth." Our help, our Rock, our Fortress, our salvation is in the Name of Jesus! St. Luke writes, "And there is salvation in no one else, for there is no other name under heaven given among men by which we must be saved." (Acts of the Apostles 4:12)

The love of God for His creatures is great; it is beyond the comprehension of the finite minds of the sinners. The Psalmist testifies to the love of God. He writes, "Praise the LORD, all nations! Extol him, all peoples! For great is his steadfast love toward us, and the faithfulness of the LORD endures forever. Praise the LORD!" (Psalm 117)

The Father is faithful to His promise because He loves us. Look for the love of the Lord in the Old Testament.

- ☐ He clothes Adam and Eve with skins of the beasts to protect them.
- ☐ He hides Noah and his family in the ark from the destruction of the world.
- ☐ He blesses Abram because of his eternal Son, the promised Messiah. By faith, Abraham received the blessing of the Lord.
- ☐ He saves Isaac by divine mercy and grace. By faith, Abraham received the blessing of Isaac's deliverance.
- ☐ He preserved the life of Joseph and Moses from death.
- ☐ He preserved the slaves in Egypt from the tenth and final plague.
- ☐ He stood with David against Goliath.
- ☐ He preserved the life of Elijah.
- ☐ He saved the lives of Shadrach, Meshach, and Abednego who trusted in the Lord.
- ☐ He saved Daniel's life in the lion's den because of His gracious protection which Daniel believed.

The Lord rescued His people countless times. He called them to repentance. He forgave them. He even went after them when they got lost and caught up in the trappings of the world. Hear again what the Lord said through the prophet Ezekiel concerning His role in caring for the sheep.

"For thus says the Lord GOD: Behold, I, *I myself will search for my sheep and will seek them out*. As a shepherd seeks out his flock when he is among his sheep that have been scattered, so will *I seek out my sheep*, and *I will rescue them from all places where they have been scattered* on a day of clouds and thick darkness. And *I will bring them out from the peoples and gather them from the countries* and will bring them into their own land. And *I will feed them on the mountains of Israel*, by the ravines, and in all the inhabited places of the country. *I will feed them with good pasture*, and on the mountain heights of Israel shall be their grazing land. There they shall lie down in good grazing land, and on rich pasture, they shall feed on the mountains of Israel. *I myself will be the shepherd of my sheep*, and *I myself will make them lie down*, declares the Lord GOD. *I will seek the lost*, and *I will bring back the strayed*, and *I will bind up the injured*, and *I will strengthen the weak*, and the fat and the strong I will destroy. I will feed them in justice." (Ezekiel 34:11-16)

The Lord did this through His Son, Jesus the Christ. Our Good Shepherd entered His creation to "seek and save the lost." (Luke 19:10) Jesus saved us and all people of all time when He suffered on our behalf and died our death. Jesus says, "I came that they may have life and have it abundantly. I am the good shepherd. The good shepherd lays down his life for the sheep." (John 10:10b-11) He gives everlasting life to all who believe on His Name.

The love of God, our Father, is revealed to us in His Son. St. Athanasius states the purpose of the Incarnation this way. He writes, "He has been manifested in a human body for this reason only, out of the love and goodness of His Father, for the salvation of us men." (On the Incarnation, 26) St. Paul says, "God demonstrates His own love toward us, in that while we were still sinners, Christ died for us." (Romans 5:8)

God did not send His Son because we are great people living great lives. He didn't send His Son because we are such great and pious people. No, He sent His Son because He loves us. St. John writes in his first epistle, "In this is love, ☐not that we loved God, but that He loved us and sent His Son ☐*to be* the propitiation for our sins." (1 John 4:10)

The world did not comprehend the Light of God in His Son, Jesus. The ears of men have heard the prophets of old but did not believe. They took this innocent man who restored sight to the blind and cleansed lepers from their disease, restored hearing to the deaf and raised the dead and preached salvation to all men and crucified Him like a common criminal.

The Roman Governor found no fault in Jesus, yet the people cried out, "Crucify, crucify Him!" (Luke 23:21) The unbelievers wanted no part of this man named Jesus who claimed to be the Son of God. Jesus' words were blasphemy to their ears. They were lost and steeped in their sin. They wanted to save their own. They wanted Barabbas.

The great thing about the story of salvation is that Jesus died to save even those who condemned Him to death. This Good News of salvation is ours to know and believe because even we turn our backs on the Lord. Ws us His gift of repentance.

The third area we want to examine is:

God's love shared through faith in the Christ.

Throughout our lives, we say to people, "I love you." We may even hear these precious words, "I love you." How do you love one another? Do you love the concept of love (thoughts)? Do you love in words alone? Do your actions back up your love with mercy for one another? The Rev. Matthew Harrison describes love this way in his pamphlet titled, "Theology for Mercy." Harrison writes, "Love, care, and concern for those in need (*diakonic* mercy/love) are actions motivated by the Gospel, when faith (*fides qua creditor*/the faith by which we believe) apprehends the righteousness of Christ and His merits (AC IV & VI), unto eternal life."[6]

Love is faith in action. Love is the fruit of the Gospel of Jesus Christ as Lord and Savior. Love is faith in action for another human being or creature of God. True love flows from faith because of the merits of Jesus and holds fast to Christ's merits and righteousness alone.

God showed His love for the world by sending His Son to atone for the sins of the world. Believing Jesus justified us in His dying for us to save us from sin, death, and the power of the devil, God's love is ours to share through faith in Jesus, our Lord and Savior.

But I ask you, what is love without action? What is faith without good works? St. James tells us:

"What *does it* profit, my brethren, if someone says he has faith but does not have works? Can faith save him? If a brother or sister is naked and destitute of daily food, and one of you says to them, "Depart in peace, be warmed and filled," but you do not give them the things which are needed for the body, what *does it* profit? Thus also faith by itself, if it does not have works, is dead. But someone will say, "You have faith, and I have works." Show me your faith without your works, and I will show you my faith by my works. You believe that there is one God. You do well. Even the demons believe—and tremble! But do you want to know, O foolish man, that faith without works is dead? Was not Abraham, our father, justified by works when he offered Isaac his son on the altar? Do you see that faith was working together with his works, and by works faith was made perfect? And the Scripture was fulfilled which says, *"Abraham believed God, and it was accounted to him for righteousness."* And he was called the friend of God. You see then that a man is justified by works, and not by faith only. Likewise, was not Rahab the harlot also justified by works when she received the messengers and sent *them* out another way? For as the body without the spirit is dead, so faith without works is dead also." (James 2:14-26)

Faith is dead without works. True love is non-existent apart from faith in Christ. Yes, unbelievers can show earthly love to family and friends but cannot show true love because they don't have faith. Love is the fruit of faith in Jesus. Love finds its source in the Triune God: Father, Son, and Holy Ghost. True love, through faith in Christ, is God's love, through Christ, expressed to one another.

When you truly love someone, your thoughts, words, and deeds are motivated by the Gospel of Jesus Christ and put into action, through faith in Christ, as you express that love in acts of mercy. To love someone is to know God through Jesus, God's Son.

MERCY

Jesus said, "Therefore be merciful, just as your Father also is merciful."
Luke 6:36

The Rich Man and Lazarus

MERCY

For even the Son of Man did not come to be served, but to serve, and to give His life a ransom for many."

Mark 10:45

In the past two Bible studies, we've examined UNITY and LOVE. We've answered the questions of whose gifts these are and the source of these gifts in Jesus the Christ. Now, in part three, we will examine the gift of mercy.

What is mercy? Simply stated, **mercy is love in action**. When we read the Gospel in a nutshell written in John 3:16, Jesus clearly describes God's mercy for the world. Jesus says, "For God so loved the world that He gave His only begotten Son, that whoever believes in Him should not perish but have everlasting life."

LOVE! Did you hear it? God loved the world. God's action of declaring you "not guilty" of your sins is because of LOVE! Hear and watch with your eyes of faith (i.e., your ears) and see God's love in action for you. Jesus continues, "…that He gave His only begotten Son…" – God shows His mercy through His Son, Jesus the Christ. Below, is the icon of God's mercy toward you when His Son, Jesus, laid down His life on the cross to save you from sin, death, and the power of the devil.

So, let us examine the Holy Scriptures for some examples of God's mercy as He serves us in our worship life in the Historic Liturgy (*Gottesdienst* – the Divine Service).

- ☐ **Mercy – Christ rescued you from the darkness.**
- ☐ **Mercy – Christ's absolution for you.**
- ☐ **Mercy – Christ's teaching to sustain the faith He created in you.**
- ☐ **Mercy – Christ's giving of His Body and Blood to you for the forgiveness of your sins.**
- ☐ **Mercy – The sharing of Christ's mercy with others.**

Many of you probably do not know of the mercy that God extended to you early on in your life. After all, we were just wee little ones in the womb. Since your conception, God has been extending His mercy to you in your life. While you were in the womb, your mother may have carried you to God's House where you heard His Word of salvation through Jesus suffering, dying, rising, and ascending.

While you were yet in the womb, the Holy Spirit then delivered to you Christ's forgiveness of sins through the very Word of God that penetrated your ears. The joy of hearing God's Word did for you in much the same way as it did for your brother, John the Baptizer. Saint Luke writes, 'And when Elizabeth heard the greeting of Mary, the baby leaped in her womb. And Elizabeth was filled with the Holy Spirit." (Luke 1:41)

Yes, even as a wee little one in the womb, you were a sinner and in need of God's mercy. In the womb, sin separated you from God. As a sinner, yes, even a wee little sinner, you only deserved the wrath of God and eternal punishment for your sin.

As a wee little creature of God, you received the richest blessings in your life through God's only-begotten Son, Jesus the Christ. The richest blessing was received when the Christ rescued you from the darkness after you came forth from the womb and blessed you with His gifts imparted through the washing of water and the Word.

Mercy – Christ rescued you from the darkness.

During the Divine Service, that is, God's service to you, The Word of God also teaches that we are all conceived and born sinful and are under the power of the devil until Christ claims us as His own. We would be lost forever unless delivered from sin, death, and everlasting condemnation. But the Father of **all mercy** and grace has sent His Son Jesus Christ, who atoned for the sin of the whole world, that whoever believes in Him should not perish but have eternal life.[7]

Did you hear the Good news? The Father of all mercy and grace sent His Son, Jesus Christ to atone for your sins that believing on the Name of Jesus, you should not perish but have eternal life. God is merciful toward you because He loves you. St. Paul writes, "…God shows his love for us in that while we were still sinners, Christ died for us." (Romans 5:8) In Christ, our Father, who is in heaven, reveals His love for the world and extends His mercy to every soul, through the death of His only-begotten Son on the cross at Calvary.

On the cross, Jesus justified you before His Father, that is, Jesus declared you not guilty of your sins. In Holy Baptism, Jesus rescued you from the darkness and wrote the Name of God upon your soul when the pastor said, "Receive the sign of the holy cross, both upon your forehead and upon your breast to mark you as one redeemed by Christ the crucified."[8] God's mercy is yours through Word and Sacrament.

As one redeemed by Christ the crucified, Jesus numbers you among the saints. You are still a sinner too. In the Church, we say that we are *simul justus et peccator*, that is, at once saint [justified] and sinner. You are in need of God's mercy and so hunger and thirst for His righteousness. (Matthew 5:6) So, you come before the Lord with contrition in your heart and cry out, "Lord, have mercy."

Mercy – Christ's absolution for you.

Christ hears your plea for mercy. He stands before you and says to you, "I forgive you all your sins in the Name of the Father and the ✠ Son and the Holy Ghost." You do nothing since Christ has already done everything for you. His mercy is yours through the Blood of the Lamb that flowed down the altar upon Calvary. The mercy of God is yours because He loves you.

One of our problems as sinners is that we love to receive the forgiveness of God for our sins but do not like exercising those same Keys with our brothers and sisters under the cross. Maybe it's due to our ignorance because we don't know what the Office of the Keys is. Maybe we know and are weak and afraid of confronting others when they transgress us. Maybe we are both ignorant and cowards.

If we don't forgive each other, then, how and why can we expect God to forgive us? Don't we pray in the Lord's Prayer, "...forgive us our trespasses as we for those who trespass against us?" We do. Do we know what we pray for in the Lord's Prayer?

There is here again the great need for us to call upon God and to pray, "Dear Father, forgive us our trespasses." It is not as though He did not forgive sin without and even before our prayer. (He has given us the Gospel, in which is pure forgiveness before we prayed or ever thought about it [Romans 5:8].) But the purpose of this prayer is that we may recognize and receive such forgiveness.[9]

We also pray for the Spirit of God to grant us the courage and strength to do God's will in sharing His forgiveness with others through Christ.

It is, therefore, the intent of this petition that God would not regard our sins and hold up to us what we daily deserve. But we pray that He would deal graciously with us and forgive, as He has promised, and so grant us a joyful and confident conscience to stand before Him in prayer [Hebrews 10:22]. For where the heart is not in a right relationship with God, or cannot take such confidence, it will not dare to pray anymore. Such a confident and joyful heart can spring from nothing else than the certain knowledge of the forgiveness of sin [Psalm 32:1–2; Romans 4:7–8]. (LC 419)

But God says this so that He may establish forgiveness as our confirmation and assurance, as a sign alongside the promise, which agrees with this prayer in Luke 6:37, "Forgive, and you will be forgiven." Therefore, Christ also repeats it soon after the Lord's Prayer, and says in Matthew 6:14, "For if you forgive others their trespasses, your heavenly Father will also forgive you," and so on.[10]

As we struggle daily with sin as Satan, the world, and our sinful flesh are always against us, we receive God's mercy in His forgiveness but also need God to sustain the faith He created in us when He Baptized us. We need His Word for the nourishment of our souls.

Mercy – Christ's teaching to sustain the faith He created in you.

During the Divine Service, our Lord Jesus serves us with three lessons from His Word. Normally, the first lesson is from the Old Testament [During Eastertide, the first lesson is from the Acts of the Apostles]. He instructs us through the lives of the saints that lived long ago. He shows us their failures because of sin. He also shows us His mercy and their reception of the same through their repentance and faith.

For instance, let us examine Numbers 21:4-9 – The Bronze Serpent event in the life of the Nation of Israel.

> "From Mount Hor they set out by the way to the Red Sea, to go around the land of Edom. And the people became impatient on the way. And the people spoke against God and against Moses, "Why have you brought us up out of Egypt to die in the wilderness? For there is no food and no water, and we loathe this worthless food." Then the LORD sent fiery serpents among the people, and they bit the people, so that many people of Israel died. And the people came to Moses and said, "We have sinned, for we have spoken against the LORD and against you. Pray to the LORD, that he take away the serpents from us." So Moses prayed for the people. And the LORD said to Moses, "Make a fiery serpent and set it on a pole, and everyone who is bitten, when he sees it, shall live." So Moses made a bronze serpent and set it on a pole. And if a serpent bit anyone, he would look at the bronze serpent and live."

What is happening here that is so important to you in 2010? What were the Israelites doing? What was Moses doing? What was God doing?

The people became impatient because God led them around the land of Edom. Impatience – isn't this sin? What sin? What commandment did they break? First and foremost, they broke the First Commandment which says, "Thou shalt have no other gods before Me." (Ex. 20:3; Is. 42:8; Matt. 4:10; 1 Cor. 8:4; 1 John 5:21) Secondly, did the Israelites covet something that the Lord had not given to them? Absolutely!

Their impatience was against God and Moses. They were sinning before God and against their brother, their neighbor, their pastor. They were committing murder before the eyes of God.

What else? What about doubt and unbelief? Were the Israelites trusting in the Lord above all things? No, they weren't. They were whining and complaining before the Lord and called His blessings "worthless."

What did the Lord do about this situation? What did He do to these sinners? He sent fiery serpents among the people and [the serpents] bit many and they died. God sent judgment on those who broke His Law and did not repent of their sins. Did God stop there? No. He heard the prayers of Moses and delivered His people. He told Moses to erect a fiery serpent and set it on a pole. God attached His promise to His word and said that everyone who bitten when he sees it, **shall live**.

The people of Israel who were bitten and looked to the bronze serpent were healed and lived.

What does this lesson mean to you in your life today? The bronze serpent is a type of the Christ. All people are bitten and infected with the venom of Satan. We are all infected with original sin. We also commit sin daily in our lives. We all will die in our iniquity unless saved from our trespasses.

What has God done for us? He raised up His banner for all to see. All who look upon the Christ and believe in Him shall not perish but have everlasting life. (John 3:14-15)

The second lesson each week comes from one of the epistles to the Church. Are these epistles still relevant today? Absolutely! I was taught long ago by a faithful pastor that if you want to read about the congregation, you attend, read Paul's epistle to the Corinthians. We are experiencing the same turmoil that the Church in Corinth experienced so long ago.

Finally, we hear the Gospel; that is the Good News from the lips of our Lord Jesus Himself. He teaches us about the salvation He came to earn for us on the cross at Calvary. We also hear His other teachings to the Church when He speaks parables. He teaches us about the miracles He did to point people to Himself. Jesus said, "If I do not do the works of My Father, do not believe Me; but if I do, though you do not believe Me, believe the works, that you may know and believe that the Father is in Me, and I in Him." (John 10:37-38)

The whole of Scripture points to the eternal Son of God. Jesus Himself said, "These are the words which I spoke to you while I was still with you, that all things must be fulfilled which were written in the Law of *Moses* and *the Prophets* and *the Psalms* concerning Me." (Luke 24:44)

Our Lord extends His mercy to us through the lessons read each week to sustain our soul. His Word is the food which the soul requires to live. Jesus also gave us His Holy Supper. He gives us this meal to eat and drink for the forgiveness of our sins. He gives us His mercy in, with, and under the bread and wine with His Body and Blood which were given and shed for us for the forgiveness of sins.

Mercy – Christ's giving of His Body and Blood to you for the forgiveness of your sins.

Christ extends His mercy to you with His Body and Blood for the forgiveness of your sins. So let's take a quick review of the Lord's Supper to learn by the heart of the promise that is ours in this holy meal.

What is the Sacrament of the Altar?
Answer: It is the true body and blood of our Lord Jesus Christ, under the bread and wine, for us Christians to eat and to drink, instituted by Christ Himself.

Where is this written?
Answer: The holy Evangelists, Matthew, Mark, Luke, and St. Paul, write:

Our Lord Jesus Christ, on the night He was betrayed, took bread, and when He had given thanks, He broke it and gave it to the disciples and said: "Take, eat; this is My body, which is given for you. This do in remembrance of Me."

In the same way also, He took the cup after supper, and when He had given thanks, He gave it to them, saying: "Drink of it, all of you; this is My blood of the new testament, which is shed for you for the forgiveness of sins. This do, as often as you drink it, in remembrance of Me."

What is the benefit of such eating and drinking?
Answer: That is shown us in these words, "Given for you" and "shed for you for the forgiveness of sins." This means that in the Sacrament forgiveness of sins, life, and salvation are given us through these words. For where there is forgiveness of sins, there is also life and salvation.

How can bodily eating and drinking do such great things?
Answer: It is not the eating and drinking, indeed, that does them, but the words, which are given here, "Given ... and shed for you, for the forgiveness of sins." These words are, besides the bodily eating and drinking, the chief thing in the Sacrament. The person who believes these words has what they say and express, namely, the forgiveness of sins.

Who, then, receives such Sacrament worthily?
Answer: Fasting and bodily preparation are, indeed, fine outward training. But a person is truly worthy and well prepared who has faith in these words, "Given ... and shed for you for the forgiveness of sins." But anyone who does not believe these words, or doubts, is unworthy and unfit. For the words "for you" require hearts that truly believe.[11]

Having been forgiven, fed with both Word and Supper, we then return thanks to the Lord with the Song of Simeon. We thank our Lord because He has shown us our salvation in the flesh on the table which He prepares before us and the face of all people. We give thanks to Him for the foretaste of the marriage feast of the Lamb which we will eat in His kingdom which has no end.

Finally, receiving the blessing of the Lord, He sends us with renewed spirits into the world to share His Good News with those around us. He sends us out to extend His mercy to the people of this world.

Mercy – The sharing of Christ's mercy with others.

Throughout His ministry, Jesus extended mercy to all kinds of people. He healed the blind (John 9:1-41). He healed the deaf (Mark 7:32-37). He healed the sick (Lk. 4:38-39; John 4:46-54). He fed the multitudes (Matt. 14:15-21, 15:32-38). He raised the dead (John 11:1-46).

Jesus did these things because He loved the people and had compassion for them. He calls us to do the same. Rev. Matthew Harrison writes the following concerning the corporate life of the Church.

The apostolic church faced similar challenges. Was the church's task "word and sacrament" or caring for the needy? *In affirming the essential nature of the church's "marks" (Gospel and Sacrament) which tell us surely where the church is present, we dare not miss the fact that love and mercy toward the needy mark the church's corporate life.* If not, it risks denial of the very Gospel and sacraments which constitute it. The apostles ordained the seven to "wait tables" (i.e. bread to the widows) that they might not "give up preaching the Word" (Acts 6:2). However, we dare never forget (at the very risk of the "destruction of the Church," says Sasse) that the apostles established a churchly office to care for the needy in its midst, and for those who came to it from without with spiritual and physical need (Gal. 6:10). From Jesus to the apostolic church, to the Missouri Synod (see Walther's "Proper Form of Christian Congregation" on caring for the poor) it has always been so. But why?

"Missions! That's it! We care to evangelize the needy! Find the need, meet it and grow the church!" I don't know about you, but I'm not happy at all with this idea. It's very pragmatic, very American, but not particularly Lutheran. Don't get me wrong. I'm convinced that the Bible teaches that eternal life is only through faith in Christ and His cross, and so evangelism is an essential part of the church's life (Matt. 28:19). But it smacks of "bait and switch" to me. Jesus proclaimed the Gospel and cared for the needy because that's who He is as mercy incarnate. Mercy responds to human need and suffering, whether spiritual or physical. The church doesn't reach out to those in need with some "whiz bang" program *because it's guaranteed to fill pews*. Proclaiming Jesus and loving the neighbor has to do with who and what the church is as the body of Christ. Where proclamation of the Gospel or acts of love and mercy are missing, the church's life is not what Christ intended it to be. Mere "social gospel" substitutes our work for Christ's. Proclamation absent love renders us a mere "clanging cymbal" (1 Corinthians 13).

Why should the church show mercy to the needy? "Simple! It's Christ's command! Love your neighbor as yourself!" This is certainly true. I don't want to minimize the importance of God's law in guiding us as His church. And yet, not only is the law not the proper motivation for Christian acts of mercy, the church shows mercy to the needy for reasons deeper than mere command. The church has a "mandate" for mercy. A "mandate" (comes from *mandatum*) is a "given" thing. The church performs acts of mercy because this is what it's given to be! A mercy place! The saints in Matthew 25 aren't even aware of how they served Christ by serving the needy!

They did these things because they were a people of mercy. Loehe (so tremendously influential in the founding of Synod, institutions of mercy, the deaconess movement, etc.) expressed this beautifully: "God's mercy (*Barmherzigkeit*) is divine love meeting need. When divine mercy meets human sin, that mercy becomes the grace of forgiveness. When divine love meets human suffering, it becomes merciful care and healing."

Why should the church care for those in need? "I'm still not convinced it should. The church should be on about preaching and the administration of the sacraments, period." You would certainly agree that every person has the mandate to be merciful to others within his/her vocation ("Here consider your station in life"). Rendering love to the neighbor is in large measure the content of the priesthood of the baptized ("Present your bodies as living sacrifices...the one who does acts of mercy, with cheerfulness" Rom. 12). So that you begin to see mercy as the church's corporate task, consider St. Paul's collection for the needy church in Jerusalem (1 Cor. 16:1ff; Acts 11:28; 2 Cor. 8:1-15; 9:12-14; and Acts 24:7). Individuals provide gifts. These gifts are collected by congregations, and even by whole "national churches" (Macedonia). More than that, they are delivered to the church in Jerusalem by none other than the Apostle Paul. This "churchly" life of mercy is expressed by Luther in the Smalcald Articles: "The church cannot be better ruled and preserved than if we all live under one head, Christ...and keep diligently together in unity of teaching, faith, sacraments, prayers, and works of love."[12] That says it all.

Luther, in fact, left us stirring descriptions of the church as a mercy place, and of its gospel-driven motivation to be merciful. The Reformer often speaks of Christ's incarnation and sacrificial death as our motivation to be merciful to the needy (including the non-believer!). He wrote to the Duke of Saxony who was ill:

> *Our Lord and Savior Jesus has left us a commandment which applies equally to all Christians, namely, that we are to render the works of mercy (Luke 6:36) to those who are afflicted, and that we are to visit the sick, try to free the captives, and do similar things for our neighbor so that the evils of the present may be somewhat lessened. Our Lord Jesus Christ himself gave us the brightest example of this commandment when, because of his infinite love for the race of men, he descended from the bosom of the Father into our misery and our prison, that is, into our flesh and our most wretched life, and took upon himself the penalty for our sins so that we might be saved. And while we have the duty to visit and console all who are afflicted with sickness, we are especially obligated to those of the household of faith."[13]*

His comments in "The Blessed Sacrament of the Holy and True Body of Christ" of 1519 (LW 35) are a "must read" to understand the church's work of mercy as part of the church's corporate life. Luther offers an antidote for an individualistic "Jesus and me" piety regarding the Lord's Supper:

There your heart must go out in love and devotion and learn that this sacrament is a sacrament of love, and that love and service are given you and you again must render love and service to Christ and His needy ones. You must feel with sorrow all the dishonor done to Christ in His holy Word, all the misery of Christendom, all the unjust suffering of the innocent, with which the world is everywhere filled to overflowing; you must fight, work, pray, and if you cannot do more, have heartfelt sympathy (LW 35:54).[14]

"You must fight, work, pray." There are no words more apt for describing the church's challenge to be a "mercy place" today. It is often very difficult for a parish to understand its life as one that receives Christ's gifts at the altar, font, and pulpit, then moves out to the world, "in fervent love for all." There has never been a more complex era for Lutheran institutions of mercy, which sorely need and want to reconnect with congregations. We as the LCMS have opportunities the world over to share Christ's mercy in word and deed—and so very much good is taking place (at the Synod level: LCMS World Relief! Institutional Chaplaincy! Housing! Life Ministries! Health Ministries! etc.). But as with all measurable things, there is so very much more need, such tremendous need to re-think and re-commit to what it means to be Lutheran and merciful, as institutions of care, and as congregations, districts, and Synod. There is a need for us to revisit and recommit to what it means for us to be Lutheran as we "cooperate in externals" with other Christians. We must not sacrifice our clear confessional and biblical Lutheran convictions even as we recognize the breadth of "one, holy, catholic and apostolic church." Where shall we find the wherewithal for the tasks at hand in this complex world?

"What do we do now, Pastor?" The usher's eyes were pleading. The entire congregation was frozen, silent. I left the altar. Soon I had extended my arm around his shoulders. "Friend, we are glad that you are here with us. Let me help you." His tension eased as I folded him into the green, Trinity season chasuble I was wearing. It was ample enough to cover us both. Not a snicker, not a smirk marked the faces of the silent observers as we made our way to the rear of the sanctuary. I handed him to others and returned to the altar. The "sacrament of love" commenced. After the service, I sought him out. He had slipped away. I never saw him again. Somehow he knew we were a "mercy place" yet to this day I have a nagging visceral disquiet about him. We failed him.

Much more ample than that chasuble that covered an unworthy servant of Christ, and a poor soul trapped by sin, death, and devil, is Holy Baptism. How shall we deal with our consciences disquieted by our failures at mercy? Where shall we find the strength of faith and fortitude as the church to be ever more what Christ has made us and called us to be: A mercy place? How shall we face the complexities of remaining faithful to our beautiful Lutheran confession in today's vexing world? Luther, no Christ himself, has an answer:

> *"We must hold boldly and fearlessly to our baptism, and hold it up against all sins and terrors of conscience, and humbly say, 'I know full well that I have not a single work which is pure, but I am baptized, and through my baptism God, Who cannot lie, has bound Himself in a covenant with me, not to count my sin against me, but to slay it and blot it out.'"* ("Treatise on Baptism," LW, Phila. Ed., 1:63).

O Lord Christ, Fount of everlasting compassion, grant Your Church on earth grace according to Your promise, that it may be the channel of your mercy to all those in need, body, and soul. And may Your merciful washing ever more beget in us merciful living.

Lord, have mercy.
Christ, have mercy.
Lord, have mercy.[15]

Peace be with you as you live under the cross of Christ receiving His mercy and extending His mercy through your Baptism.

WITNESS

Jesus said, ""Therefore whoever confesses Me before men, him I will also confess before My Father who is in heaven. ³³ But whoever denies Me before men, him I will also deny before My Father who is in heaven."
Matthew 10:32-33

The Reverend Doctor Martin Luther

"Unless I am convinced by Scripture and plain reason - I do not accept the authority of the popes and councils, for they have contradicted each other - my conscience is captive to the Word of God. I cannot and I will not recant anything for to go against conscience is neither right nor safe. God help me. Amen."

WITNESS

For there are three that bear witness in heaven: the Father, the Word, and the Holy Spirit; and these three are one. And there are three that bear witness on earth: the Spirit, the water, and the blood; and these three agree as one.   1 John 5:7-8

Over the past couple of months, we've discussed Unity,

Love, and Mercy. We now come to Witness. This study will complete the new emphasis of President Harrison this year.

What does witness mean? It means to attest to a fact or an event. Testimony is another word for witness. To be a witness is to be one that gives evidence specifically before a judicial authority. A witness is also someone who is asked to be present at transactions of importance to testify that the transaction took place. A witness is someone who has personal knowledge of something or someone. A witness is someone who gives public affirmation by word or example usually about religious faith or conviction.

So, let's not waste any time and let's jump into the Holy Writ and see what God is teaching us about WITNESS.

Let's take a look at WITNESS in the following ways:
- legal accounts
- confessional accounts
- blood accounts

LEGAL ACCOUNTS

First, legal accounts. In the Old Testament, there are numerous accounts of legal witnesses. Let's take a look at a few of them.

Ruth 4:7-12 – This account relates the redemption of a field from Naomi by Boaz.

> Now this was the custom in former times in Israel concerning redeeming [buying back] and exchanging: to confirm a transaction, the one drew off his sandal and gave it to the other, and this was the manner of ***attesting*** in Israel. So when the redeemer said to Boaz, "Buy it for yourself," he drew off his sandal. Then Boaz said to the elders and all the people, "***You are witnesses*** [Μάρτυρες] [עֵדִים] this day that I have bought from the hand of Naomi all that belonged to Elimelech and all that belonged to Chilion and to Mahlon. Also Ruth the Moabite, the widow of Mahlon, I have bought to be my wife, to perpetuate the name of the dead in his inheritance, that the name of the dead may not be cut off from among his brothers and from the gate of his native place. ***You are witnesses*** [μάρτυρες] [עֵדִים] this day." Then all the people who were at the gate and the elders said, "***We are witnesses*** [Μάρτυρες] [עֵדִים]. May the LORD make the woman, who is coming into your house, like Rachel and Leah, who together built up the house of Israel. May you act worthily in Ephrathah and be renowned in Bethlehem, and may your house be like the house of Perez, whom Tamar bore to Judah, because of the offspring that the LORD will give you by this young woman."

Isaiah 8:1-2 – Isaiah found "reliable witnesses" concerning a property title written on a large tablet.

> Then the LORD said to me, 'Take a large tablet and write on it in common characters, 'Belonging to Maher-shalal-hash-baz.' And I will get ***reliable witnesses*** [μάρτυράς] [עֵדִים], Uriah the priest and Zechariah the son of Jeberechiah, to attest for me."

Jeremiah 32:6-15 – To confirm the prophecy of the return of the exiles from Babylon, Jeremiah bought and paid for a field in the presence of witnesses, who also signed the deed for the property.

> Jeremiah said, "The word of the LORD came to me: Behold, Hanamel the son of Shallum your uncle will come to you and say, 'Buy my field that is at Anathoth, for the right of redemption by purchase is yours.' Then Hanamel my cousin came to me in the court of the guard, in accordance with the word of the LORD, and said to me, 'Buy my field that is at Anathoth in the land of Benjamin, for the right of possession and redemption is yours; buy it for yourself.' Then I knew that this was the word of the LORD. "And I bought the field at Anathoth from Hanamel my cousin, and weighed out the money to him, seventeen shekels of silver. I signed the deed, sealed it, got ***witnesses*** [עֵדִים], and weighed the money on scales. Then I took the sealed deed of purchase, containing the terms and conditions and the open copy. And I gave the deed of purchase to Baruch the son of Neriah son of Mahseiah, in the presence of Hanamel my cousin, in the presence of the ***witnesses*** [עֵדִים] who signed the deed of purchase, and in the presence of all the Judeans who were sitting in the court of the guard. I charged Baruch in their presence, saying, 'Thus says the LORD of hosts, the God of Israel: Take these deeds, both this sealed deed of purchase and this open deed, and put them in an earthenware vessel, that they may last for a long time. For thus says the LORD of hosts, the God of Israel: Houses and fields and vineyards shall again be bought in this land.'

CONFESSIONAL ACCOUNTS

Let's read 1 John 4:12-16.

No one has ever seen God; if we love one another, God abides in us and his love is perfected in us. By this, we know that we abide in him and he in us because he has given us of his Spirit. And we have seen and testify that the Father has sent his Son to be the Savior of the world. Whoever **confesses** [ὁμολογήσῃ - from the root ὁμολογέω]] that Jesus is the Son of God, God abides in him, and he in God. So we have come to know and to believe the love that God has for us. God is love, and whoever abides in love abides in God, and God abides in him.

Here our Lord is teaching us that μαρτυρέω (testify/witness) is synonymous with ὁμολογέω [confess]. The first part of ὁμολογέω is ὁμο [homo]. Homo means the same. The second part of ὁμολογέω is λογέω [to say a thing].

Let's compare these two words with the actions of John the Baptist in the Gospel According to Saint John. Let's read John 1:19-20.

And this is the **testimony** [μαρτυρία]of John when the Jews sent priests and Levites from Jerusalem to ask him, "Who are you?" He **confessed** [ὡμολόγησεν], and did not deny, but **confessed** [ὡμολόγησεν], "I am not the Christ."

Hear again, the purpose for which John the Baptist was sent [John 1:7]:

He came as a **witness** [μαρτυρίαν], to bear **witness** [μαρτυρήσῃ] about the light, that all might believe through him.

One of the greatest examples of the witness [*martyria*] is God Himself in John 1:1-5. Let's listen.

"In the beginning was the Word, and the Word was with God, and the Word was God. He was in the beginning with God. All things were made through him, and without him was not anything made that was made. In him was life, and the life was the light of men. The light shines in the darkness, and the darkness has not overcome it."

The one true God, Father, Son, and Holy Ghost testifies here that He was in the beginning. You remember these famous words; they are the words that God opens His writing of the Holy Writ in Genesis 1:1-2.

Another place where we learn of a great witness is in 1 John 5:7-8.

For there are three that bear **witness** [μαρτυροῦντες] in heaven: the Father, the Word, and the Holy Spirit; and these three are one. And there are three that bear **witness** on earth: the Spirit, the water, and the blood; and these three agree as one. (NKJV)

For there are three that testify: the Spirit and the water and the blood; and these three agree. (ESV)

Note: v 7b-8 was added by Erasmus in 1522 (his 3rd edition of the Greek text). Erasmus removed this in his 4th edition of the Greek text. This is known as the Johannine comma.

Listen to what the Church Fathers say concerning this passage in the Holy Scriptures[16]

CLEMENT OF ALEXANDRIA writes about the saving powers: The spirit is life, the water is regeneration and faith, the blood is knowledge, and these three are one. In the Savior these are the saving powers, and life itself is found in the Son.

BEDE writing about what the Spirit attests: When the Lord was baptized in the Jordan, the Spirit descended on him in the form of a dove, bearing witness that he is the truth, that he is the true Son of God, that he is the true Mediator between God and humanity, that he is the true Redeemer and Reconciler of the human race, that he is truly free from any contamination of sin, that he is truly able to take away the sins of the world.

AUGUSTINE writes about the Spirit, the Water and the Blood: What was it that flowed from Jesus' side if not the sacrament which believers receive? The Spirit, the blood and the water—the Spirit which he gave up, the blood and water which flowed from his side. The church is signified as being born from this blood and water.

LEO THE GREAT writes about The Witnesses Distinct Yet Not Separated: This means the Spirit of sanctification, the blood of redemption and the water of baptism, which three are one and remain distinct, and none of them is separated from union with the others. This is the faith by which the church lives and moves.

As we discuss and learn about μαρτυρέω (testify/witness) and ὁμολογέω [confess], we will learn about our WITNESS/CONFESSION as our Lord teaches us in these three ways:
- ☐ Confession of sins
- ☐ Confession of faith
- ☐ Confession of praise

Confession of sins

First, let's look at the confession of sins. Let's turn to Matthew chapter three. Here, Saint Matthew writes for us the account of John the Baptist during his ministry in the wilderness. What is John preaching? He preaches repentance. Why? He is preparing the way of the Lord. He is calling people to repent of their sins and preparing them to receive the Christ and the gifts He brings.

You see, when the Pharisees and Sadducees came to John, he barked at them, "Brood of vipers! Who warned you to flee from the wrath to come?" (Matthew 3:7) John is referring to the wrath that comes on the Day of Judgment. To flee the wrath is to repent of your sins and believe in Jesus Christ as Lord and Savior. St. Paul writes to the Church in Thessalonica, "…and to wait for his Son from heaven, whom he raised from the dead, Jesus who delivers us from the wrath to come." (1 Thessalonians 1:10)

If we remain steeped in our sin, we do not abide in Christ. If we deny our sins, we deny the Christ. St. John writes in his First Epistle, "If we say we have no sin, we deceive ourselves, and the truth is not in us." (1 John 1:8) Jesus says, "…but whoever denies me before men, I also will deny before my Father who is in heaven." (Matthew 10:33) What is the antonym of denying? It is to confess, witness, bear testimony.

The death of sinners is not the desire of God. God's desire is "...all people to be saved and to come to the knowledge of the truth." (1 Timothy 2:4) He sent His only-begotten Son to atone for the sin of the world. The sacrifice of the Lamb of God on the cross was not a selective atonement. Jesus died to atone for all sin of all mankind, past, present, and future. God takes no pleasure in the death of the wicked. He says to us through the prophet Ezekiel, "Do I have any pleasure at all that the wicked should die?" says the Lord GOD, "and not that he should turn [repent/confess] from his ways and live [absolution]?" (Ezekiel 18:23)

The God of all mercy hears our confession and gives us His grace through His Son, Jesus Christ. His promise to forgive our sins is true. He tells us, "If we confess [ὁμολογέω] our sins, he is faithful and just to forgive us our sins and to cleanse us from all unrighteousness." (1 John 1:9) The Lord promises the forgiveness of sins. He says, "'Come now, and let us reason together,' says the LORD, 'Though your sins are like scarlet, They shall be as white as snow; Though they are red like crimson, They shall be as wool.'" (Isaiah 1:18)

Enough for now about the confession of sins. Let's talk now about our second point which is the confession of faith.

Confession of faith

What are we talking about when we speak of confessing the faith? St. Paul writes, "There is one body and one Spirit, just as you were called in one hope of your calling; one Lord, one faith, one baptism." (Ephesians 4:4-5) St. Paul writes, "one faith." The one faith that Paul writes about is faith in Jesus, the eternal and only-begotten Son of God. This "one faith" in Ephesians 4 is the true Christian faith as confessed in a summary way in the Creed.

When we speak of confessing the faith, we, as sinners, can say nothing of our volition. As Christians, the words we speak to confess Jesus Christ as Lord are given to us by God Himself as He has revealed His Son to us in His written Word.

The writer to the Hebrews writes, "Seeing then that we have a great High Priest who has passed through the heavens, Jesus the Son of God, let us hold fast our confession." (Hebrews 4:14)

Our confession [ὁμολογέω] before God, one another, and the world is to say again [ὁμολογέω] what God has already said to us in His Word about Himself and His Son, Jesus Christ. St. Paul writes it this way in his Epistle to Rome, "But what does it say? "The word is near you, in your mouth and in your heart" (that is, the word of faith which we preach): that if you confess with your mouth the Lord Jesus and believe in your heart that God has raised Him from the dead, you will be saved. For with the heart one believes unto righteousness, and with the mouth confession is made unto salvation. (Romans 10:8-10)

We, as Christians, as members of Christ's Bride, the Church, use three different Creeds to confess [ὁμολογέω] the Christian faith. We use the Apostles' Creed, the Nicene Creed, and the Athanasian Creed. When we confess [ὁμολογέω] the Christian faith, in Christ Jesus, we bear witness [μαρτυρέω] to the One true God: Father, Son, and Holy Ghost.

As Lutherans in the Missouri Synod, the confession of faith begins with the pronoun "I" because no other person can confess the faith for you. You must believe and confess with your mouth that which is in your heart (soul). The faith of another is powerless to save another.

The Creeds of the Christian Church "…teach us to know Him [God] fully" [Ephesians 3:19]. We cannot know God apart from Jesus. Jesus reveals the Father to us in His flesh and in His written Word (the Bible is God's written revelation).

That is enough for now. We will reserve the in-depth teaching of the Christian doctrine for another day. Let's turn our attention now to the third part, the Confession of Praise.

Confession of praise

What is this confession of praise you ask? It is our confession before God with praise and thanksgiving on our lips. Our worship life is confessional. During worship we confess [ὁμολογέω], that is, say the same thing, and we confess [μαρτυρέω], that is, bear witness to God with our voices in song and our lips with thanksgiving.

When we examine our worship life, our confession [μαρτυρέω] begins with the Invocation. Every Divine Service begins, "In the Name of the Father and of the ✠ Son and of the Holy Ghost" to which the Church responds "**AMEN.**"

During the Divine Service, we sing praises to God in the highest with the Gloria in Excelsis and other Canticles. Our Confession of Praise continues with the singing of the Alleluia's before the pastor proclaims the Gospel lesson. Of course, our Confession of Praise is confessed with the Creed every week giving thanks to God for all He does for us out of His Fatherly, divine, goodness, and mercy.

After the sermon, the preached Word of God, we praise His holy Name with the Offertory as we come to Him, as His Children, with humble requests for the soul. Our Confession of Praise continues in the Liturgy of the Sacrament with the song of the seraphim, "Holy, holy, holy, Lord God of Sabaoth; heaven and earth are full of Thy glory. Hosanna, hosanna, hosanna in the highest."

After we receive the Body and Blood of our Lord Jesus Christ, which were given and shed for us for the forgiveness of sins, we praise God for this holiest gift with the Song of Simeon. We then return thanks to God, as we do after every meal, for the blessings, He has bestowed upon us. This sacrifice of praise and thanksgiving is also Gottesdienst, i.e., our service to God because of His service to us. Gottesdienst can run two ways – first, God's service to us (primary) and second, our service in turn to God (secondary).

Is Church attendance important? Absolutely. The writer to the Hebrews writes:

"Therefore, brethren, having boldness to enter the Holiest by the blood of Jesus, by a new and living way which He consecrated for us, through the veil, that is, His flesh, and having a High Priest over the house of God, let us draw near with a true heart in full assurance of faith, having our hearts sprinkled from an evil conscience and our bodies washed with pure water. Let us hold fast the confession of our hope without wavering, for He who promised is faithful. *And let us consider one another in order to stir up love and good works, not forsaking the assembling of ourselves together, as is the manner of some, but exhorting one another, and so much the more as you see the Day approaching.*" (Hebrews 10:19-25)

When you search the Holy Scriptures for words or phrases like, "praise the Lord," "rejoice," "sing," you will mine treasure upon treasures about our worship life as Christians who bear the Name of the Trinity. Let's take a look at a few:

Genesis 29:35	And she conceived again and bore a son, and said, "Now I will **praise the LORD**." Therefore she called his name Judah. Then she stopped bearing.
Ezra 3:10	When the builders laid the foundation of the temple of the LORD, the priests stood in their apparel with trumpets, and the Levites, the sons of Asaph, with cymbals, to **praise the LORD**, according to the ordinance of David, King of Israel.
Psalm 7:17	I will **praise the LORD** according to His righteousness And will **sing** praise to the name of the LORD Most High.
Psalm 33:1-3	*Rejoice* in the LORD, O you righteous! For *praise* from the upright is beautiful. ***Praise the LORD*** with the harp; Make melody to Him with an instrument of ten strings. ***Sing*** to Him a new song; Play skillfully with a shout of joy.
Psalm 106:1	***Praise the LORD!*** Oh, give thanks to the LORD, for He is good! For His mercy endures forever. *(This one should sound real familiar!)*
Deuteronomy 12:7	And there you shall eat before the LORD your God, and you shall ***rejoice*** in all to which you have put your hand, you and your households, in which the

	LORD your God has blessed you.
Deuteronomy 26:11	So you shall ***rejoice*** in every good thing which the LORD your God has given to you and your house, you and the Levite and the stranger who is among you.
Job 21:12	They ***sing*** to the tambourine and harp, and ***rejoice*** to the sound of the flute.
Psalm 13:5	But I have trusted in Your mercy; My heart shall ***rejoice*** in Your salvation.
Psalm 33:1	***Rejoice*** in the LORD, O you righteous! For ***praise*** from the upright is beautiful.
Matthew 2:10	When they saw the star, they ***rejoiced*** with exceedingly great joy.
Luke 15:9	And when she has found it, she calls her friends and neighbors together, saying, '***Rejoice*** with me, for I have found the piece which I lost!'
Romans 5:11	And not only that, but we also ***rejoice*** in God through our Lord Jesus Christ, through whom we have now received the reconciliation.
Philippians 2:16	holding fast the word of life, so that I may ***rejoice*** in the day of Christ that I have not run in vain or labored in vain.
Exodus 15:1	Then Moses and the children of Israel ***sang*** this song to the LORD, and spoke, saying: "I will ***sing*** to the LORD, For He has triumphed gloriously! The horse and its rider He has thrown into the sea!
1 Chronicles 16:9	***Sing*** to Him, ***sing*** psalms to Him; Talk of all His wondrous works!
1 Chronicles 16:23	***Sing*** to the LORD, all the earth; Proclaim the good news of His salvation from day to day.
Psalm 9:11	***Sing*** praises to the LORD, who dwells in Zion! Declare His deeds among the people.
Acts 16:25	But at midnight Paul and Silas were praying and ***singing*** hymns to God, and the prisoners were listening to them.
Ephesians 5:19	speaking to one another in psalms and hymns and spiritual songs, ***singing*** and making melody in your heart to the Lord

The writer to the Hebrews says it best, "Therefore by Him let us continually offer the sacrifice of praise to God, that is, the fruit of our lips, giving thanks to His name." (Hebrews 13:15)

Let us never cease bringing our Confession of Praise before the Lord God Almighty. Let ever be faithful to Him who loves us and is merciful to us for the sake of His only-begotten Son, Jesus Christ.

That is enough for now. As we conclude this section, we must remember that our WITNESS [μαρτυρέω] and confession [ὁμολογέω] are given to us through faith in Jesus Christ, our Lord, and Savior. As we learn by heart, not just memorizing, but learning for life, we remember that our trust, our faith is in the First true Apostle sent by God our Father who is our Lord Jesus.

Jesus testifies about the Father that He and the Father are One. (John 10:30) Jesus testifies of Himself: "I am One who bears witness of Myself, and the Father who sent Me bears witness of Me." (John 8:18) The Spirit testifies of Jesus: "But when the Helper comes, whom I shall send to you from the Father, the Spirit of truth who proceeds from the Father, He will testify of Me." (John 15:26)

St. John writes, "For there are three that bear witness in heaven: the Father, the Word, and the Holy Spirit; and these three are one. And there are three that bear witness on earth: the Spirit, the water, and the blood; and these three agree as one." (1 John 5:7-8)

We've covered the first two accounts of WITNESS; Legal and Confessional. Let's take a look now at the third and final part of our study, the blood accounts.

BLOOD ACCOUNTS

When we speak of a testimony of blood, we are usually speaking of martyrdom. Martyr's are people who die because of their confession of Jesus.

In the Acts of the Apostles, St. Luke writes about the death of Stephen. (Acts 7:57-60) James, the brother of John, the son of Zebedee, was killed by Herod. (Acts 12:2) Eusebius writes, "First; Stephen was stoned to death by them, and after him, James, the son of Zebedee and the brother of John, was beheaded..."[17]

Andrew is believed to have been crucified at Patrae; this is according to Hippolytus.

Hippolytus identifies James, the son of Alphaeus, being stoned to death in Jerusalem.

Eusebius records that Peter was put to death under Nero in Rome. "It is, therefore, recorded that Paul was beheaded in Rome itself and that Peter likewise was crucified under Nero. This account of Peter and Paul is substantiated by the fact that their names are preserved in the cemeteries of that place even to the present day."[18]

According to Hippolytus, Philip preached and was executed in what today is eastern Turkey. "Philip preached in Phrygia, and was crucified in Hierapolis with his head downward in the time of Domitian, and was buried there."

Hippolytus records that Thomas was an active missionary and that he met his fate in India. "And Thomas preached to the Parthians, Medes, Persians, Hyrcanians, Bactrians, and Margians, and was thrust through in the four members of his body with a pine spear at Calamene, the city of India, and was buried there."

Hippolytus was martyred around A.D. 236.

Young Perpetua, a catechumen learning the doctrine of Holy Scripture, and her slave girl, Felicitas, were beheaded for converting to Christianity. These martyrs died around A.D. 202.

The Rev. Dr. Martin Luther wrote a song called, "A New Song Now Shall Be Begun." He wrote this ballad about the lives of Heinrich Voes and Johann Esch who were burned at the stake for the Name of Jesus.

Sadly, there are still people today, in 2011, being killed for the Gospel of Jesus Christ.

As we conclude our study of WITNESS, the Holy Scriptures teach us that as we witness and bear testimony [μαρτυρέω] of our Lord Jesus, the faith we confess [ὁμολογέω] drives us to extend the love and mercy of God to those around us.

Peace be with you as you continue to "Fight the good fight of faith, lay hold on eternal life, to which you were also called and have confessed the good confession in the presence of many witnesses." (1 Timothy 6:12)

FORGIVENESS

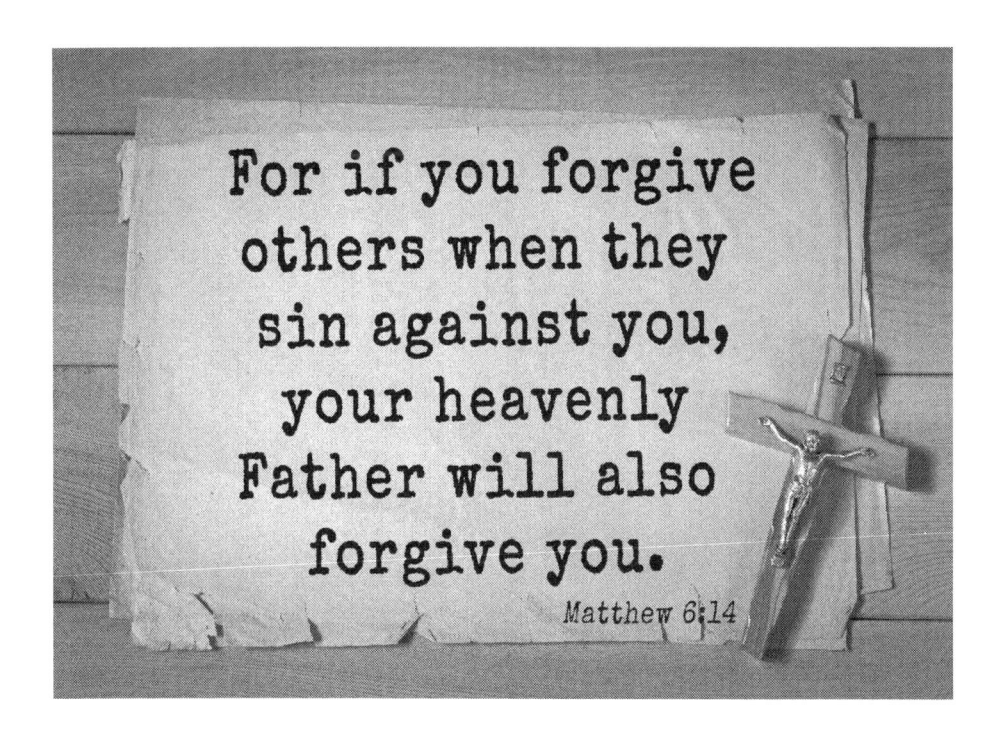

> For if you forgive others when they sin against you, your heavenly Father will also forgive you.
>
> Matthew 6:14

Then Peter came to Him and said, "Lord, how often shall my brother sin against me, and I forgive him? Up to seven times?"
- Matthew 18:19

FORGIVENESS

I have discussed with you some very important topics concerning the life of the Christian. You learned about Unity, that is Life Together, and how your life is in the crucified and risen Lord Jesus. You learned about Love and how the love you have and share is not your love but God's love to you through faith in Jesus Christ. Next, you learned about Mercy and how mercy is love in action, but not just any love but God's love in action to you in your life and then as you share it through faith with your neighbor. Last month, you learned about Witness. You learned what it means to bear witness, that is, to testify before the world of the Son of God, Jesus Christ, who died to atone for your sins and the sins of the world. You learned about confessing the Name of Jesus and all that He has already done for you in His Incarnation, birth, preaching and teaching, miracles, suffering, death, resurrection, and ascension. Now, we come to another great pillar in the Holy Scriptures called Forgiveness. Let us turn our eyes of faith (your ears) to the Holy Writ and hear what Jesus says about forgiveness.

As we mine the Scriptures, let's look at the following:

- ☐ **Why do you need forgiveness?**
- ☐ **What is this thing called repentance?**
- ☐ **How are you forgiven?**
- ☐ **Are you supposed to forgive?**

Let's get busy. Why do you need forgiveness? Is forgiveness something only Christians need or is this for all people?

Forgiveness is for all people; men, women, and children too. You need forgiveness. You want forgiveness. Without forgiveness, you are lost and condemned because of your sins.

The need for forgiveness stemmed from disobedience. You understand disobedience. About 6,000+ years ago, after God finished creating the world and all that is in it and declared everything to be very good, He rested. Adam and Eve were tending to the Garden in Eden. Everything was going along great. Then, one fateful day, the devil approached the woman and asked her, "Has God indeed said, 'You shall not eat of every tree of the garden'?" (Gen. 3:1b) He was tricky. He disguised himself so he would be recognized. Then, he asked a simple question. The question is tempting because it requires the human to recall what God said to them. The question begs the human to trust in God above all things. Eve answered the devil's question. She did well too until she made a huge mistake. Eve responded, "...but of the fruit of the tree which is in the midst of the garden, God has said, 'You shall not eat it, nor shall you touch it, lest you die.' " (Gen. 3:3) Eve added to the Word. Once the devil heard this, he knew he had her. Eve sinned. Eve broke God's Law (νόμος). Sin is lawlessness. Sin is iniquity. Sin is a transgression. Sin is opposition and disobedience. Sin is punishable, and God stated that the punishment is death if Adam and Eve ate from the Tree of Knowledge of Good and Evil.

When Eve, and Adam too, disobeyed God and His Word, they brought sin and death into God's creation. Mankind died spiritually that fateful day. Sin severed the relationship between God and man. Man in his sin now stood in opposition to God. Because the first Adam disobeyed God, man needs a Savior; a Savior that will pay the price for man's sin and restore sinners back to God by His sacrifice.

In the modern world in which we live today, most people do not recognize themselves to be sinners and thus have no need for forgiveness. People today think they live good lives. They don't hurt anyone. They don't steal, murder, or even swear. They think highly of themselves. They are gods among men. They are powerful and can do no wrong. Forgiveness – it's overrated. Or is it?

St. John writes in his first Epistle, "If we say that we have no sin, we deceive ourselves, and the truth is not in us. If we confess our sins, He is faithful and just to forgive us our sins and to cleanse us from all unrighteousness. If we say that we have not sinned, we make Him a liar, and His word is not in us." (1 John 1:8-10)

In verse 8, John says, "If we say that we have no sin, we deceive ourselves, and the truth is not in us." We lie to ourselves. Sinners lie. Lying is what idolaters do. They make up the rules to suit themselves so they can do whatever they want in this life. John also says at the end of the verse that when you set yourself up as a god and live in deceit, the truth is not in you. Truth – what is truth? The truth is Christ Jesus, God's only begotten Son. Jesus says, "I am the way, the truth, and the life. No one comes to the Father except through Me." (John 14:6)

You cannot say I believe in Jesus and say you are not a sinner. You are a liar and a hypocrite. A sinner who confesses Jesus Christ as Lord and Savior recognizes his sin and thus falls on his face and cries out, "Lord, have mercy." The sinner who believes in Jesus for his salvation knows he cannot save himself. Those who say they can are liars and deceivers.

St. Paul writes in his Epistle to the Church in Rome, "Therefore we conclude that a man is justified by faith apart from the deeds of the law." (Rom. 3:28) To be justified is to be declared righteous. Justification is being declared not guilty before God the Father because of His Son, Jesus.

You need forgiveness for your sins. Without God's forgiveness, the sinner will die in iniquity. You will deserve your just reward on Judgment Day which is God's wrath and His punishment for your sins which is death. Jesus forgives you. He doesn't count your sins against you. When He forgives you, your sins are forgotten as far as the east is from the west. (Psalm 103:12) You need God's forgiveness to live.

Are you thinking to yourself, "Alright, you now have my attention." I get it. I am a sinner. I need forgiveness. How do I get it? What is this thing called repentance?

Repentance is turning away from sin and returning to righteousness. Repentance involves changing the mind of the sinner. Repentance often involves reverting from idolatry to true worship of Yahweh and its corresponding moral behavior (Isa. 1:10–17; Ezek. 14:6; 18:30; Amos 4:6–11). Let's look at these four accounts.

First, Isaiah 1:10-17:

"Hear the word of the LORD, You rulers of Sodom; Give ear to the law of our God, You people of Gomorrah: "To what purpose is the multitude of your sacrifices to Me?" Says the LORD. "I have had enough of burnt offerings of rams and the fat of fed cattle. I do not delight in the blood of bulls, or of lambs or goats. "When you come to appear before Me, Who has required this from your hand, to trample My courts? Bring no more futile sacrifices; Incense is an abomination to Me. The New Moons, the Sabbaths, and the calling of assemblies— I cannot endure iniquity and the sacred meeting. Your New Moons and your appointed feasts My soul hates; They are a trouble to Me, I am weary of bearing them. When you spread out your hands, I will hide My eyes from you; even though you make many prayers, I will not hear. Your hands are full of blood. "Wash yourselves, make yourselves clean; Put away the evil of your doings from before My eyes. Cease to do evil, Learn to do good; Seek justice, Rebuke the oppressor; Defend the fatherless; Plead for the widow."

Next, Ezekiel 14:6:

"Therefore say to the house of Israel, 'Thus says the Lord GOD: "Repent, turn away from your idols, and turn your faces away from all your abominations."

Now, Ezekiel 18:30:

"Therefore I will judge you, O house of Israel, every one according to his ways," says the Lord GOD. "Repent, and turn from all your transgressions, so that iniquity will not be your ruin."

Finally, Amos 4:6-11

> "Also I gave you cleanness of teeth in all your cities. And lack of bread in all your places; Yet you have not returned to Me," Says the LORD. "I also withheld rain from you, when there were still three months to the harvest. I made it rain on one city, I withheld rain from another city. One part was rained upon, And where it did not rain the part withered. So two or three cities wandered to another city to drink water, But they were not satisfied; Yet you have not returned to Me," Says the LORD. "I blasted you with blight and mildew. When your gardens increased, Your vineyards, Your fig trees, And your olive trees, The locust devoured them; Yet you have not returned to Me," Says the LORD. "I sent among you a plague after the manner of Egypt; Your young men I killed with a sword, Along with your captive horses; I made the stench of your camps come up into your nostrils, Yet you have not returned to Me," Says the LORD. "I overthrew some of you, As God overthrew Sodom and Gomorrah, And you were like a firebrand plucked from the burning, Yet you have not returned to Me," Says the LORD."

Listen to Jesus. Hear Him. He explains the reason He came to earth. Let's turn to Luke 5:27-32.

> "After these things, He went out and saw a tax collector named Levi, sitting at the tax office. And He said to him, 'Follow Me.' So he left all, rose up, and followed Him. Then Levi gave Him a great feast in his own house. And there were a great number of tax collectors and others who sat down with them. And their scribes and the Pharisees complained against His disciples, saying, 'Why do You eat and drink with tax collectors and sinners?' Jesus answered and said to them, 'Those who are well have no need of a physician, but those who are sick. I have not come to call the righteous, but sinners, to repentance.'"

Jesus came to save sinners. He came to heal them of their disease (sin) by granting to those who believe in Him the forgiveness of their sins. Jesus' forgiveness is healing. It is restoration. It is God's gift of mercy, that is, forgiveness is God's love in action toward the sinner.

Jesus came preaching repentance. Peter, Paul, and the other disciples did the same. They all preached repentance. Why? If the sinner ignores the Word of God and ignores the law of God, the sinner dies in iniquity. Jesus sends His pastors out to preach repentance. The Word of God changes the minds of arrogant sinners. Man cannot change the mind of a sinner. Man cannot convince anyone he is doing wrong. Only God can turn the heart of the wicked.

Hear what Jesus says concerning repentance. "And He said, "What comes out of a man, that defiles a man. For from within, out of the heart of men, proceed evil thoughts, adulteries, fornications, murders, thefts, covetousness, wickedness, deceit, lewdness, an evil eye, blasphemy, pride, foolishness. All these evil things come from within and defile a man." (Mark 7:20-23)

As you can see, there is nothing good in man. Without God's help, man could not repent. God is the one who turns the heart of man from evil to good. God works in your life to bring you to know Him and to confess your sins. Yes, repentance is the change in man. A changed man is one who believes in Jesus as Lord and Savior. God's forgiveness restores the sinner and makes alive that which was dead and lost.

Alright then, I am a poor miserable sinner. I know I cannot save myself. How am I forgiven? Forgiveness is yours from God and your neighbor. Before forgiveness, you must acknowledge your sin by confessing it, that is, saying it out loud to God or to the neighbor you offended.

In his Small Catechism, Martin Luther explains Confession this way:

How Christians should be taught to confess
[The practice of Confession and Absolution is from Mt 16:19; 18:15; etc.]

What is Confession?[19]
Confession has two parts.

First, that we confess our sins, and second, that we receive absolution, that is, forgiveness, from the pastor as from God Himself, not doubting, but firmly believing that by it our sins are forgiven before God in heaven.

What sins should we confess?

Before God we should plead guilty of all sins, even those we are not aware of, as we do in the Lord's Prayer; but before the pastor, we should confess only those sins which we know and feel in our hearts.

Which are these?

Consider your place in life according to the Ten Commandments: Are you a father, mother, son, daughter, husband, wife, or worker? Have you been disobedient, unfaithful, or lazy? Have you been hot-tempered, rude, or quarrelsome? Have you hurt someone by your words or deeds? Have you stolen, been negligent, wasted anything, or done any harm?

What is the Office of the Keys?

The Office of the Keys is that special authority which Christ has given to His church on earth to forgive the sins of repentant sinners but to withhold forgiveness from the unrepentant as long as they do not repent.

Where is this written?

This is what St. John the Evangelist writes in chapter twenty: The Lord Jesus breathed on His disciples and said, **"Receive the Holy Spirit. If you forgive anyone his sins, they are forgiven; if you do not forgive them, they are not forgiven."** [Jn 20:22–23]

What do you believe according to these words?

I believe that when the called ministers of Christ deal with us by His divine command, in particular when they exclude openly unrepentant sinners from the Christian congregation and absolve those who repent of their sins and want to do better, this is just as valid and certain, even in heaven, as if Christ our dear Lord dealt with us Himself. (SC V)

St. Paul instructs us to examine our lives especially before the reception of the Lord's Supper. When you turn to God's Word for such an examination, the Christian often stumbles because he/she doesn't know how or what to ask themselves about how they have transgressed their Lord and their neighbor.

To help you in your Christian life, I am providing you some questions to help "prick" your conscience as you examine your living against the Word of God. The Rev. Dr. Kenneth Korby, of The Lutheran Church-Missouri Synod, prepared the following questions for self-examination. He left them for the Church to use before his death in 2006.

A Form for Self-examination before Confession based on the Holy Ten Commandments[20]

THE FIRST COMMANDMENT

You shall have no other gods.

What does this mean? We should fear, love, and trust in God above all things.

My God is that which I love, trust, and fear most in my life. I expect my comfort, good, and delight from God.

Have I loved, trusted, or feared other things or people more than I love, trust, and fear God?

Have I committed idolatry by seeking comfort, good, and delight from my own efforts rather than from God?

Do I look to God my heavenly Father for all love, good, and joy?

Is everything measured by what pleases me?

In all things am I self-centered and selfish?

Have I patiently borne the afflictions God sends me?

Have I doubted whether human affairs are ruled by God's counsel?

Have I been angry that the wicked seem to enjoy a better lot than the pious and that the pious are often oppressed?

Do I see my worry and fretting as sin against trusting in God?

On what things is my attention focused?

Do I complain about the troubles, people, work and suffering God lays on me?

Do I love the things God gives more than I love Him?

Do I cling to what God takes away, even though He gives me Himself?

THE SECOND COMMANDMENT

You shall not misuse the name of the Lord your God.

What does this mean? We should fear and love God so that we do not curse, swear, use satanic arts, lie or deceive by His name, but call upon it in every trouble, pray, praise, and give thanks.

My God has placed His name upon me in Holy Baptism and made me His dearly beloved child through my Lord Jesus Christ. In His name, He has revealed Himself to me as the God of love that I might worship Him.

Have I cursed?

Have I used God's name cheaply for oaths that are frivolous or false?

Do I stand up and swear by God's name when it is for the truth of the Gospel or the benefit of my neighbor in need?

Have I doubted whether God hears my prayer?

Do I seek my own glory or God's glory?

Do I pray with fervor in times of trouble?

Am I bored and indifferent in prayer?

Am I unable to speak about God truly because I am bored with His Word and have neglected the study of the catechism and doctrine?

Is my heart in the praise I speak with my lips?

Do I speak praise with my lips?

Am I thankful for the blessings God showers on me?

Do I use my lips to complain?

THE THIRD COMMANDMENT

Remember the Sabbath day by keeping it holy.

What does this mean? We should fear and love God so that we do not despise preaching and His Word but hold it sacred and gladly hear and learn it.

My God has given me His Word so that I might know Him and believe in Him. His Word makes me holy. It gives me eternal life and rest from all my enemies.

Do I strive to make the day of rest holy by making time for the hearing of God's Word and the reception of the Sacrament?

Do I care about holy living?

Have I put the desires of my body ahead of the needs of my soul?

Do I use the Word of God to make my time, work, study, and life holy day by day?

Have I doubted the truth of God's Word?

Am I lazy about reading and studying God's Word?

Have I any fear of God over this neglect?

Do I honor the Word of God highly by eagerly hearing it preached at the appointed times?

Do I gladly learn it by heart and live in it?

Do I despise God's Word by not paying attention when it is read, preached on, or taught in Church?

Do I love my fellow Christians by being present with them in the divine liturgy to sustain them?

Am I quick to make excuses for neglecting the divine liturgy to do other things I like more?

Have I absented myself from the divine liturgy because I was angry at someone else who was there?

Do I complain about the worship, the pastor, or other people in the congregation?

Do I learn the Word of God gladly so that I can teach it to others?

THE FOURTH COMMANDMENT

Honor your father and your mother.

What does this mean? We should fear and love God so that we do not despise or anger our parents and other authorities, but honor them, serve and obey them, love and cherish them.

My God has given me my father and mother through whom I received life from Him. He has placed them and all temporal authority over me for my good and for the benefit of my neighbor.

Has the fear and love of God shaped my honor and obedience to parents and others in authority over me?

Have I trusted God to bless me in my life and make my life good when I submit to the authority of parents and those over me?

Have I been angry with them, rebelling and fighting with them, because I was not getting what I wanted?

Have I talked back to those in authority over me?

Have I disobeyed their commands or obeyed them only with complaining?

Have I been disrespectful and sullen to my parents, teachers, employers, or other authorities over me?

Have I been on good behavior in their presence while mocking them or disobeying them when they are absent, pretending that God does not see this rebellion?

Have I prayed for my parents, my pastor, my schools, my government?

Do I grumble about work that is given me to do?

THE FIFTH COMMANDMENT

You shall not murder.

What does this mean? We should fear and love God so that we do not hurt or harm our neighbor in his body, but help and support him in every physical need.

My God has given me and all people life. Our life is holy because God created us in His image to receive what He gives and to reflect His love to one another.

Have I treated my neighbor's body and life as gifts God has given to him?

Have I injured my neighbor with violent actions, hitting and beating my neighbor?

Have I spoken debasing and insulting words to my neighbor?

Have I used foul or dirty words to describe my neighbor?

Have I murdered him in my heart with thoughts of anger, contempt, and hatred?

Have I injured my neighbor by ridicule?

Have I neglected to feed, clothe and care for my neighbor in his need?

Have I avoided giving help to my neighbor?

Do I abuse my own body with excessive use of food, drink, alcohol or drugs?

Have I been tempted to commit suicide as though my life were my own to end?

Have I aborted a baby or approved of the practice of abortion?

THE SIXTH COMMANDMENT

You shall not commit adultery.

What does this mean? We should fear and love God so that we live a sexually pure and decent life in what we say and do, and husband and wife love and honor each other.

My God has given me the gift of sexuality that I might love and honor my spouse selflessly and for the procreation of children.

Have I used for my own pleasure my ears to hear stories that incite cravings of the body for one who is not my spouse?

Have I used my mouth to tell such stories?

Have I indulged my eyes with longing for my sexual satisfaction from a man or woman who is not my spouse?

Have I dishonored marriage by ridicule, divorce, or neglecting to encourage others to be faithful to their spouses in the fear of God?

Have I had sexual intercourse with a man or woman not my spouse?

Have I dishonored my spouse by neglecting to care for my spouse's body, mind, feelings, and needs, withdrawing faithfulness from my spouse?

Have I failed to trust God to bless us in our marriage, even in times of trouble?

Have I neglected to pray for my spouse, to attend the divine liturgy together, and to live in the fear and love of God in times of sexual temptation?

Have I used pornography?

Have I engaged in homosexual thoughts, word, or deeds, or given approval to homosexual activity?

Have I given approval to those who live together apart from marriage?

THE SEVENTH COMMANDMENT

You shall not steal.

What does this mean? We should fear and love God so that we do not take our neighbor's money or possessions, or get them in any dishonest way, but help him to improve and protect his possessions and income.

My God has given me my property and goods that I might serve my family and neighbor with His gifts.

Have I been lazy at work, doing poor work in school or at my job, or working only when the teacher or boss is around?

Have I been stingy in paying my workers?

Have I been greedy, demanding best pay for poor work?

Have I worked for myself rather than for Christ and for the benefit of my neighbor?

Have I cared for property in the neighborhood, church, and school so that it is improved?

Have I stolen from office, school, church, or from my neighbor?

Have I stood by silently while others took what was not theirs?

Have I stolen information from another's work?

Have I wasted time, food, and money by my neglect?

Have I been stingy when it comes to giving to the Lord a generous portion as a thank offering for all He has given to me?

Have I stolen from my neighbor by not helping him in time of need?

THE EIGHTH COMMANDMENT

You shall not give false testimony against your neighbor.

What does this mean? We should fear and love God so that we do not tell lies about our neighbor, betray him, slander him, or hurt his reputation; but defend him, speak well of him, and explain everything in the kindest way.

My God has given me a good name and reputation that I might cover my neighbor's sins and short-comings with mercy, in order to preserve his name and reputation in the community.

Have I told the truth in court, or in school before authorities, or before my parents when I knew the truth?

Have I been afraid to bear witness when I knew the truth and it was necessary to speak up against a wrongdoer or to speak for a victim?

Have I told lies?

Have I passed on information my neighbor shared with me about himself in confidence?

Have I gossiped, delighting to tell others about the faults or mistakes of another, excusing myself especially by saying that I only spoke the truth?

Have I gone to others to make peace if I wronged them or they me?

Have I flattered others?

Have I put on a front to make others think differently of me than I am?

Have I slanted stories to my benefit or to deceive others by withholding some elements of the truth?

Have I found ways gladly and willingly to explain in the kindest way those words or actions of others that hurt me?

Have I defended my neighbor when he is criticized by others?

Have I learned to bear with faults and weaknesses of others, covering their shame?

THE NINTH COMMANDMENT

You shall not covet your neighbor's house.

What does this mean? We should fear and love God so that we do not scheme to get our neighbor's inheritance or house, or get it in a way which only appears right, but help and be of service to him in keeping it.

My God has given me everything that I need and all that is good for me.

Have I longed for the honor, wealth, happy life, or what seems like the ease of others?

Has my life been full of craving for things that are not mine?

Have I been stingy or self-indulgent with my money, trying to keep up with what others have?

Have I tried by claims of various rights to make the property of others my own?

Do I have to keep wishing for and dreaming about things I don't have before I can work with a joyful heart?

Have I resented the blessings God has given to my neighbor?

Have I thought that happiness comes from owning things?

Have I been generous?

THE TENTH COMMANDMENT

You shall not covet your neighbor's wife, or his manservant or maidservant, his ox or donkey, or anything that belongs to your neighbor.

What does this mean? We should fear and love God so that we do not entice or force away our neighbor's wife, workers, or animals, or turn them against him, but urge them to stay and do their duty.

My God has given me Himself. He is my God. His will is good and gracious. In Him I am content.

Have I wanted my neighbor's spouse, his workers, or property to be mine?

Have I tried to win the affections and loyalties of my neighbor's spouse or children away from my neighbor to me?

Have I urged friends, spouses, and workers to go back to their callings, holding their marriages, friendships and work together?

Have I fostered discontent with the congregation, its pastors or leaders, and failed to urge members to stay and do their duty in the divine liturgy: praying, giving and serving?

CLOSE OF THE COMMANDMENTS

What does God say of all these commandments?
He says: I, the Lord your God, am a jealous God, punishing the children for the sins of the fathers to the third and fourth generation of those who hate me, but showing love to a thousand generations of those who love me and keep my commandments.

What does this mean? God threatens to punish all who break these commandments, therefore we should fear His wrath and not do anything against them. But He promises grace and mercy to all who keep these commandments, therefore we should also love and trust in Him and gladly do what He commands.

Lord, have mercy upon us.
Christ, have mercy upon us.
Lord, have mercy upon us.

The Rev. Dr. Laurence L. White provides the following in his book, Life with God. The following material comes from the section on The Office of the Keys.[21]

Repentance - The Crucial Issue

The critical issue in all this is repentance. In Scripture, repentance (Greek - *"metanoia"*) indicates a radical change of heart and mind followed by a moral and behavioral reformation of sinful life. *"Metanoia"* is a very powerful word which implies a fundamental coming to one's self (Luke 15:10), in which the sinner, by the power of the Holy Spirit, becomes intensely aware of sin as an offense to divine holiness and comes to loathe the power of sin within his life. One then turns away from sin in grief over the misdeeds that have been done and turns toward God, seeking pardon and forgiveness. Repentance is part and parcel of the daily reality of the Christian life. In the first of his famous *"95 Theses"* Martin Luther declares: *"When our Lord and Master Jesus Christ said, "Repent!" (Matthew 4:17) he willed the entire life of believers to be one of repentance."* Psalm 51, the great Penitential Psalm of King David after his sin with Bathsheba, is the Bible's classic statement of personal repentance. In the magnificent words of the Psalm, David abandons all pretense of personal justification, acknowledges the enormity of his offense against the holiness of God, and casts himself upon the mercy of his heavenly Father.

It was a pastoral concern over the crucial issue of personal repentance which triggered the Reformation. As one of the priests of the City Church in Wittenberg, Martin Luther had been assigned the responsibility to hear the confessions of the members of his parish and pronounce forgiveness to the penitent. When he discovered that his people believed that it was no longer necessary for them to repent because they had purchased indulgences from John Tetzel, he warned them that without personal repentance their sins could not be forgiven and refused to grant them absolution. He proceeded to attack the entire theology of indulgences as destructive of men's souls. The rest, as they say, is history.

Gustav Koenig, a 19th Century German artist, demonstrates the connection between these events in an engraving on the historic posting of the 95 theses. Luther is depicted at the center of the image, posting the theses against indulgences on the door of the Castle Church in Wittenberg. To his left is John Tetzel, the infamous indulgence seller, offering the purchase of forgiveness. To his right, the people of Wittenberg cast the worthless indulgences into the fire after their pastor has led them to understand that it is impossible to buy the forgiveness of sins. At the bottom of the engraving, Luther is shown hearing confession, and refusing to grant forgiveness to those who are not truly penitent. With these events the Protestant Reformation began. The crucial issue was repentance! The great preacher and theologian St. John Chrysostom distinguishes the following five components in genuine repentance.

REPENTANCE

1. **Recognition and Acknowledgment of Sin**
2. **Contrition (Sorrow for Sin)**
3. **Seek Forgiveness in Christ**
4. **Conscientious Resolve Not to Repeat the Sin**
5. **Willingness, Wherever Possible, to Undo the Damage of the Sin**

"When our Lord and Master Jesus Christ said, 'Repent' (Matthew 4:17), He willed the entire life of believers to be one of repentance...Any truly repentant Christian has a right to full remission of penalty and guilt, even without indulgence letters...The true treasure of the Church is the most holy gospel of the glory and grace of God...Christians should be exhorted to be diligent in following Christ, their Head, through penalties, death, and hell; and thus be confident of entering into heaven through many tribulations rather than through the false security of peace."

(Martin Luther, from the ***"95 Theses"*** - 1517)

Christian Discipline

When a brother or sister in Christ is living in manifest impenitent sin the community of God's people is obligated to implement the process of Christian discipline. The motive in this process must always be humble, Christlike love which earnestly desires the restoration of the brother. While the permissive culture in which we live may scorn such action as judgmental and self-righteous, true love cannot look the other way when someone we care about is involved in a pattern of self-destructive behavior. A church which fails to practice Christian discipline has failed to demonstrate genuine love to fellow believers in need. At the same time, a failure to practice Christian discipline undermines the integrity of our witness both to our own members and to the world around us.

The steps in the process of Christian Discipline are clearly delineated by our Lord Himself in Matthew Chapter 18. The goal of each step in the process is to lead the sinner to repentance. When that goal has been achieved, the process is joyfully discontinued.

Steps In the Process of Christian Discipline (Matthew 18)

1. Private, individual contact with the sinner (vs.15)
2. Contact with one or two witnesses (vs. 16)
3. Tell it to the church (vs. 17)
4. Excommunication (vs. 17)

Excommunication - Tough Love In Action

When all else fails, in one final desperate attempt to bring the sinner to his senses, so that he may come to recognize the dire spiritual peril into which he has placed himself, the church resorts to excommunication (Matthew 18:17; 1 Corinthians 5:1-13; Titus 3:10-11). A decree of excommunication is the formal pronouncement by the church that because of persistent impenitence an individual who has failed to respond in all of the steps in the process of Christian discipline is no longer a believer. The excommunicant is expelled from the fellowship of the church and may no longer participate in the Lord's Supper. He is literally *ex communio* (Latin – *outside of the communion*). He is no longer a Christian and if he persists in his impenitence until death, he will not be saved. In the ancient church, the grim significance of excommunication was dramatically conveyed with the symbolism of the bell, the book, and the candle.

When an excommunication was announced the church bell was tolled as for the dead to indicate that the excommunicant was spiritually dead. The chancel Bible was closed to represent the removal of the individual's name from the Book of Life in heaven.

Finally, one of the altar candles was extinguished to show that the light of faith had gone out within the impenitent sinner's heart. If excommunication achieves its desired result, the sinner will recognize and repent of his sin and be restored to the fellowship of the church.
(1 Corinthians 5:5; 2 Corinthians 2:5-11)

Are you supposed to forgive others? Let us hear the Word of God.

Jesus says in His instructions on how to pray, "And forgive us our debts, As we forgive our debtors." (Matt. 6:12)

Jesus continues with His teaching, "For if you forgive men their trespasses, your heavenly Father will also forgive you. But if you do not forgive men their trespasses, neither will your Father forgive your trespasses." (Matt. 6:14-15)

Jesus teaches how important forgiveness is in the life of the Christian. Hear Him. "Then Peter came to Him and said, "Lord, how often shall my brother sin against me, and I forgive him? Up to seven times?" Jesus said to him, "I do not say to you, up to seven times, but up to seventy times seven. (Matt. 18:21-22)

And again, "Take heed to yourselves. If your brother sins against you, rebuke him; and if he repents, forgive him. And if he sins against you seven times in a day, and seven times in a day returns to you, saying, 'I repent,' you shall forgive him." (Luke 17:3-4)

Here now the words of St. Paul to the Church in Ephesus. "Let all bitterness, wrath, anger, clamor, and evil speaking be put away from you, with all malice. And be kind to one another, tenderhearted, forgiving one another, even as God in Christ forgave you." (Eph. 4:31-32)

Forgiveness is an act of love through faith in Jesus Christ. Love keeps no record of wrongs. (1 Cor. 13:5) Love covers a multitude of sins. (1 Peter 4:8) Finally, Jesus Himself reminds us to forgive one another. Hear His words as St. Mark wrote them, "And whenever you stand praying, if you have anything against anyone, forgive him, that your Father in heaven may also forgive you your trespasses." (Mark 11:25)

"For God so loved the world that He gave His only begotten Son, that whoever believes in Him should not perish but have everlasting life." (John 3:16) God's love for you sent His Son to die for you to forgive you all your sins.

"Therefore be imitators of God as dear children. And walk in love, as Christ also has loved us and given Himself for us, an offering and a sacrifice to God for a sweet-smelling aroma." (Eph. 5:1-2)

Peace be with you.

Let us pray.

Almighty God, merciful Father, in Your mercy so guide the course of this world that we may forgive as we have been forgiven and joyfully serve You in godly peace and quietness; through Jesus Christ, Thy dear Son, our Lord, who lives and reigns with Thee and the Holy Ghost, one true God, world without end. **Amen.**

Endnotes

[1] Well then, the Children's Creed teaches us (as was said) that a Christian holy people is to be and to remain on earth until the end of the world. This is an article of faith that cannot be terminated until that which it believes comes, as Christ promises, "I am with you always, to the close of the age" [Matt. 28:20]. But how will or how can a poor confused person tell where such Christian holy people are to be found in this world? Indeed, they are supposed to be in this life and on earth, for they of course believe that a heavenly nature and an eternal life are to come, but as yet they do not possess them. Therefore they must still be in this life and remain in this life and in this world until the end of the world. For they profess, "I believe in another life"; thereby they confess that they have not yet arrived in the other life, but believe in it, hope for it, and love it as their true fatherland and life, while they must yet remain and tarry here in exile—as we sing in the hymn about the Holy Spirit, "As homeward we journey from this exile. Lord, have mercy." We shall now speak of this.

First, the holy Christian people are recognized by their possession of the holy word of God. To be sure, not all have it in equal measure, as St. Paul says [I Cor. 3:12–14]. Some possess the word in its complete purity, others do not. Those who have the pure word are called those who "build on the foundation with gold, silver, and precious stones"; those who do not have it in its purity are the ones who "build on the foundation with wood, hay, and straw," and yet will be saved through fire. More than enough was said about this above. This is the principal item, and the holiest of holy possessions, by reason of which the Christian people are called holy; for God's word is holy and sanctifies everything it touches; it is indeed the very holiness of God, Romans 1 [:16], "It is the power of God for salvation to every one who has faith," and I Timothy 4 [:5], "Everything is consecrated by the word of God and prayer." For the Holy Spirit himself administers it and anoints or sanctifies the Christian church with it rather than with the pope's chrism, with which he anoints or consecrates fingers, garb, cloaks, chalices, and stones. These objects will never teach one to love God, to believe, to praise, to be pious. They may adorn the bag of maggots, but afterward they fall apart and decay with the chrism and whatever holiness it contains, and with the bag of maggots itself.

Yet this holy possession is the true holy possession, the true ointment that anoints unto life eternal, even though you cannot have a papal crown or a bishop's hat, but must die bare and naked, just like children (in fact, all of us), who are baptized naked and without any adornment. But we are speaking of the external word, preached orally by men like you and me, for this is what Christ left behind as an external sign, by which his church, or his Christian people in the world, should be recognized. We also speak of this external word as it is sincerely believed and openly professed before the world, as Christ says, "Every one who acknowledges me before men, I also will acknowledge before my Father and his angels" [Matt. 10:32]. There are many who know it in their hearts, but will not profess it openly. Many possess it, but do not believe in it or act by it, for the number of those who believe in and act by it is small—as the parable of the seed in Matthew 13 [:4–8] says that three sections of the field receive and contain the seed, but only the fourth section, the fine and good soil, bears fruit with patience.

Now, wherever you hear or see this word preached, believed, professed, and lived, do not doubt that the true *ecclesia sancta catholica*, "a Christian holy people" must be there, even though their number is very small. For God's word "shall not return empty," Isaiah 55 [:11], but must have at least a fourth or a fraction of the field. And even if there were no other sign than this alone, it would still suffice to prove that a Christian, holy people must exist there, for God's word cannot be without God's people, and conversely, God's people cannot be without God's word. Otherwise, who would preach or hear it preached, if there were no people of God? And what could or would God's people believe, if there were no word of God?

This is the thing that performs all miracles, effects, sustains, carries out, and does everything, exorcises all devils, like pilgrimage-devils, indulgence-devils, bull-devils, brotherhood-devils, saint-devils, mass-devils, purgatory-devils, monastery-devils, priest-devils, mob-devils, insurrection-devils, heresy-devils, all pope-devils, also Antinomian-devils, but not without raving and rampaging, as is seen in the poor men mentioned in Mark 1 [:23–26] and 9 [:17–29]. No, he must depart with raving and rampaging as is evidenced by Emser, Eck,[388] Snot-nose, Schmid,[390] Wetzel, Bumpkin, Boor, Churl, Brute, Sow, Ass, and the rest of his screamers and scribes. They all are the devil's mouths and members, through whom he raves and rampages. But it does them no good. He must take his leave; he is unable to endure the power of the word. They themselves confess that it is God's word and Holy Scripture, claiming, however, that one fares better with the fathers and the councils. Let them go their way. It is enough for us to know how this chief holy possession purges, sustains, nourishes, strengthens, and protects the church, as St. Augustine also says, "The church is begotten, cared for, nourished, and strengthened by the word of God."[393] But those who persecute and condemn it identify themselves by their own fruits.

Second, God's people or the Christian holy people are recognized by the holy sacrament of baptism, wherever it is taught, believed, and administered correctly according to Christ's ordinance. That too is a public sign and a precious, holy possession by which God's people are sanctified. It is the holy bath of regeneration through the Holy Spirit [Titus 3:5], in which we bathe and with which we are washed of sin and death by the Holy Spirit, as in the innocent holy blood of the Lamb of God. Wherever you see this sign you may know that the church, or the holy Christian people, must surely be present, even if the pope does not baptize you or even if you know nothing of his holiness and power—just as the little children know nothing of it, although when they are grown, they are, sad to say, estranged from their baptism, as St. Peter laments in II Peter 2 [:18], "They entice with licentious passions of the flesh men who have barely escaped from those who live in error," etc. Indeed, you should not even pay attention to who baptizes, for baptism does not belong to the baptizer, nor is it given to him, but it belongs to the baptized. It was ordained for him by God, and given to him by God, just as the word of God is not the preacher's (except in so far as he too hears and believes it) but belongs to the disciple who hears and believes it; to him is it given.

Third, God's people, or Christian holy people, are recognized by the holy sacrament of the altar, wherever it is rightly administered, believed, and received, according to Christ's institution. This too is a public sign and a precious, holy possession left behind by Christ by which his people are sanctified so that they also exercise themselves in faith and openly confess that they are Christian, just as they do with the word and with baptism. And here too you need not be disturbed if the pope does not say mass for you, does not consecrate, anoint, or vest you with a chasuble. Indeed, you may, like a patient in bed, receive this sacrament without wearing any garb, except that outward decency obliges you to be properly covered. Moreover, you need not ask whether you have a tonsure or are anointed. In addition, the question of whether you are male or female, young or old, need not be argued—just as little as it matters in baptism and the preached word. It is enough that you are consecrated and anointed with the sublime and holy chrism of God, with the word of God, with baptism, and also this sacrament; then you are anointed highly and gloriously enough and sufficiently vested with priestly garments.

Moreover, don't be led astray by the question of whether the man who administers the sacrament is holy, or whether or not he has two wives. The sacrament belongs to him who receives it, not to him who administers it, unless he also receives it. In that case he is one of those who receives it, and thus it is also given to him. Wherever you see this sacrament properly administered, there you may be assured of the presence of God's people. For, as was said above of the word, wherever God's word is, there the church must be; likewise, wherever baptism and the sacrament are, God's people must be, and vice versa. No others have, give, practice, use, and confess these holy possessions save God's people alone, even though some false and unbelieving Christians are secretly among them. They, however, do not profane the people of God because they are not known; the church, or God's people, does not tolerate known sinners in its midst, but reproves them and also makes them holy. Or, if they refuse, it casts them out from the sanctuary by means of the ban and regards them as heathen, Matthew 18 [:17].

Fourth, God's people or holy Christians are recognized by the office of the keys exercised publicly. That is, as Christ decrees in Matthew 18 [:15–20], if a Christian sins, he should be reproved; and if he does not mend his ways, he should be bound in his sin and cast out. If he does mend his ways, he should be absolved. That is the office of the keys. Now the use of the keys is twofold, public and private. There are some people with consciences so tender and despairing that even if they have not been publicly condemned, they cannot find comfort until they have been individually absolved by the pastor. On the other hand, there are also some who are so obdurate that they neither recant in their heart and want their sins forgiven individually by the pastor, nor desist from their sins. Therefore the keys must be used differently, publicly and privately. Now where you see sins forgiven or reproved in some persons, be it publicly or privately, you may know that God's people are there. If God's people are not there, the keys are not there either; and if the keys are not present for Christ, God's people are not present. Christ bequeathed them as a public sign and a holy possession, whereby the Holy Spirit again sanctifies the fallen sinners redeemed by Christ's death, and whereby the Christians confess that they are a holy people in this world under Christ. And those who refuse to be converted or sanctified again shall be cast out from this holy people, that is, bound and excluded by means of the keys, as happened to the unrepentant Antinomians.

You must pay no heed here to the two keys of the pope, which he converted into two skeleton keys to the treasure chests and crowns of all kings. If he does not want to bind or reprove sin, whether it be publicly or privately (as he really does not), let it be reproved and bound in your parish. If he will not loose, or forgive it, let it be loosed and forgiven in your parish, for his retaining or binding, his remitting or releasing, makes you neither holy nor unholy, since he can only have skeleton keys, not the true keys. The keys belong not to the pope (as he lies) but to the church, that is, to God's people, or to the holy Christian people throughout the entire world, or wherever there are Christians. They cannot all be in Rome, unless it be that the whole world is there first—which will not happen in a long time. The keys are the pope's as little as baptism, the sacrament, and the word of God are, for they belong to the people of Christ and are called "the church's keys" not "the pope's keys."[397]

Fifth, the church is recognized externally by the fact that it consecrates or calls ministers, or has offices that it is to administer. There must be bishops, pastors, or preachers, who publicly and privately give, administer, and use the aforementioned four things or holy possessions in behalf of and in the name of the church, or rather by reason of their institution by Christ, as St. Paul states in Ephesians 4 [:8], "He received gifts among men …"—his gifts were that some should be apostles, some prophets, some evangelists, some teachers and governors, etc. The people as a whole cannot do these things, but must entrust or have them entrusted to one person. Otherwise, what would happen if everyone wanted to speak or administer, and no one wanted to give way to the other? It must be entrusted to one person, and he alone should be allowed to preach, to baptize, to absolve, and to administer the sacraments. The others should be content with this arrangement and agree to it. Wherever you see this done, be assured that God's people, the holy Christian people, are present.

It is, however, true that the Holy Spirit has excepted women, children, and incompetent people from this function, but chooses (except in emergencies) only competent males to fill this office, as one reads here and there in the epistles of St. Paul that a bishop must be pious, able to teach, and the husband of one wife—and in I Corinthians 14 [:34] he says, "The women should keep silence in the churches." In summary, it must be a competent and chosen man. Children, women, and other persons are not qualified for this office, even though they are able to hear God's word, to receive baptism, the sacrament, absolution, and are also true, holy Christians, as St. Peter says [I Pet. 3:7]. Even nature and God's creation makes this distinction, implying that women (much less children or fools) cannot and shall not occupy positions of sovereignty, as experience also suggests and as Moses says in Genesis 3 [:16], "You shall be subject to man." The gospel, however, does not abrogate this natural law, but confirms it as the ordinance and creation of God.

Here the pope will object through his loudmouths and brawlers of the devil, saying, "St. Paul does not speak only of pastors and preachers, but also of apostles, evangelists, prophets, and other high spiritual vocations; that is why there must be higher vocations in the church than those of pastors and preachers. What, Sir Luther, do you have to say now?" What do I have to say now? This is what I have to say: if they themselves would become apostles, evangelists, prophets, or would show me at least one among them—oh, what nonsense I am talking!—who is worth as much as a schoolboy or who is as well versed in Holy Scripture and in Christian doctrine as a seven-year-old girl, I shall declare myself caught. Now I know for certain that an apostle, an evangelist, a prophet knows more, or indeed as much, as a seven-year-old girl. (I am speaking about Holy Scripture and about faith.) For I thoroughly believe, more firmly than I believe in God, that they are acquainted with more human doctrine, and also with more villainy, because they are proving it before my very eyes by the things they are doing, and so they are apostles, evangelists, and prophets just as little as they are the church; that is to say, they are the devil's apostles, evangelists, and prophets. The true apostles, evangelists, and prophets preach God's word, not against God's word.

Now, if the apostles, evangelists, and prophets are no longer living, others must have replaced them and will replace them until the end of the world, for the church shall last until the end of the world [Matt. 28:20]. Apostles, evangelists, and prophets must therefore remain, no matter what their name, to promote God's word and work. The pope and his followers, who persecute God's word while admitting that it is true, must be very poor apostles, evangelists, and prophets, just like the devil and his angels. But why do I keep coming back to these shameful, filthy folk of the pope? Let them go again, and bid them not to return, or etc.

Just as was said earlier about the other four parts of the great, divine, holy possession by which the holy church is sanctified, that you need not care who or how those from whom you receive it are, so again you should not ask who and how he is who gives it to you or has the office. For all of it is given, not to him who has the office, but to him who is to receive it through this office, except that he can receive it together with you if he so desires. Let him be what he will. Because he is in office and is tolerated by the assembly, you put up with him too. His person will make God's word and sacraments neither worse nor better for you. What he says or does is not his, but Christ, your Lord, and the Holy Spirit say and do everything, in so far as he adheres to correct doctrine and practice. The church, of course, cannot and should not tolerate open vices; but you yourself be content and tolerant, since you, an individual, cannot be the whole assembly or the Christian holy people.

But you must pay no attention to the pope, who bars any married man from being called to such an office. With Nestorian logic he declares that all must be chaste virgins; that is to say, all the clergy must be chaste, while they themselves may, of course, be unchaste. But look here! You bring up the pope again, and yet I did not want you any more. Well then, unwelcome guest that you are, I will receive you in Luther-like fashion.

The pope condemns the marriage of bishops or priests; that is now plain enough. Not content with that, he condemns bigamy even more severely. Indeed, to express myself clearly, he distinguishes four, if not five, kinds of bigamy.[402] I will now call one who marries twice or who takes another's widow to wife a bigamist. The first kind of bigamist is one who marries two virgins successively; the second, one who marries a widow; the third, one who marries the betrothed whose deceased groom left her a virgin. The fourth acquires the name shamefully because he is the one who marries a "virgin," unknowingly or unwillingly, and later discovers that she is not at all pure or a virgin. And yet, in the pope's judgment this person must be more of a bigamist than the third type who married the virgin bride. All of these men stink and have an evil smell in canon law. They are not allowed to preach, baptize, administer the sacrament, or hold any office in the church, even if they were holier than St. John and their wives holier than the mother of God. So marvelously holy is the pope in his decretals!

However, if someone had ravished a hundred virgins, violated a hundred honorable widows, and lain with a hundred whores before that, he may become not only pastor or preacher but also bishop or pope. And even if he were to continue this kind of life, he would nonetheless be tolerated in those offices. But if he marries a bride who is a virgin, or a make-believe virgin, he cannot be a servant of God. It makes no difference that he is a true Christian, learned, pious, competent. He is a bigamist; thus, he must leave his office and never return to it. What do you think of that? Is that not a higher holiness than that of Christ himself, together with that of the Holy Spirit and his church? Christ spurns neither men with one wife or two successive wives, nor women with one husband or two successive husbands, if they believe in him. He lets them remain members of his holy, Christian people. He also make use of them for whatever work they are adapted. Scripture uses the term "bigamist" for one who, like Lamech, has two wives living at the same time [Gen. 4:19]. The pope, however, is more learned and calls one who marries two women successively a bigamist. He applies the same rule to women, for he is far more learned than God himself.

Better still, the pope himself admits that a bigamous marriage is a true marriage and does not constitute a sin against God, nor against the world or the church, and that such a marriage is a sacrament of the church; and yet such a man must be barred from holding an ecclesiastical office—as must the third or fourth type of bigamists, who really should be called husbands of one wife or husbands of virgins. Why? Well, here is the rub: such a marriage cannot be a sacrament or an image of Christ and his church, for Christ had but one bride, the church, and this bride has but one husband, Christ, and both remain virgins. So much sheer nonsense has been talked about this subject that it is impossible to relate it at all. The canonists should rightly be called lawyers for asses. First, if marriage is to be a sacrament of Christ and his church, then no marriage can be a sacrament unless both bridegroom and bride remain virgin, for Christ and the church remain virgins. But how will we get children and heirs under those conditions? What will become of the estate of marriage, instituted by God? In summary, there will be no marriage, other than that of Mary and Joseph and others like it. All the remaining marriages cannot be a sacrament, and may perhaps even be harlotry.

Second, who taught or decreed this, that we must keep it? St. Paul says (they say) in Ephesians 4 [5:31–32] that husband and wife are a great sacrament. I say, "Yes, in Christ and the church." My dear man, can you gather from these words of St. Paul that marriage is the kind of a sacrament of which they speak? He says that husband and wife are one body, which is a great sacrament. Then he interprets himself, saying, "I speak of Christ and the church, not of husband and wife." But they say that he is speaking of husband and wife. Paul envisages Christ and the church as a great sacrament or "mystery"; so they say that husband and wife are a great sacrament. Why then do they regard it as virtually the least of the sacraments, indeed, as sheer impurity and sin, in which one cannot serve God? Moreover, can you also deduce from St. Paul's words that men and women in bigamous marriages are not husband and wife or one body? If they are one body, why then are they not a sacrament of Christ and the church? After all, St. Paul is speaking generally about husbands and wives who become one body, whether they were single or widowed before, and calls them a sacrament (as you understand "sacrament"). Whence then are you so clever as to differentiate in marriage, taking only the single marriage as a sacrament of Christ and the church—that is, the marriage of a man with a virgin—and excluding all others? Who ordered you to martyr and force St. Paul's words in this manner?

Furthermore, you do not even call such a marriage a sacrament. For bridegrooms do not let their brides remain virgins, nor do the latter marry men in order that they may stay virgins; this they could do far better without husbands. No, they want and should bear children, for which God created them. What now becomes of the sacrament of Christ and the church, both of whom remained virgins? Is this the best argument "from image to historical fact or, conversely, from historical fact to image?" Where did you learn such logic? Christ and the church are married, but remain virgins in the body; therefore husband and wife shall also remain virgins in the body. Furthermore, Christ is married to only one virgin; therefore a Christian or a priest shall also be married to only one virgin; otherwise, you say, there is no sacrament. Why, then, do you admit and say that the marriage of a widow is also a sacrament because it is a marriage, and again it is not a sacrament because the wife was not a virgin? Are you not mad, and crazy, and crass Nestorians, not knowing when you say yes and when you say no, stating one thing in the premise and another in the conclusion? Away with you stupid asses and fools!

Another crass error stemmed from the fact (unless, indeed, the former grew out of this) that they called and regarded bishops and popes as the bridegrooms of the church. In verification of this view they cite the saying of St. Paul, "A bishop must be the husband of one wife" [I Tim. 3:2], that is to say, he must be the bishop of one church, as Christ is the bridegroom of one church; therefore they should not be bigamists. Popes and bishops, indeed, are fine fellows to be bridegrooms of the church—yes, if she were a brothel-keeper or the devil's daughter in hell. True bishops are servants of this bride, and she is lady and mistress over them. St. Paul calls himself *diaconus*, a "servant of the church" [I Cor. 3:5]. He does not claim to be the bridegroom or the lord of this bride, rather, the true and only bridegroom of this bride is called Jesus Christ, God's Son. St. John does not say, "I am the bridegroom," but, "I am the friend of the bridegroom, who stands and hears him, and who rejoices greatly at the bridegroom's voice," for "he who has the bride" (he says) "is the bridegroom" [John 3:29]. One should gladly give ear to such speech and then conduct oneself as a servant.

But how nicely they themselves keep even this crass asininity and folly.

A bishop may have three bishoprics, and yet he must be called husband of one wife. And even if he has but one bishopric, he still has one hundred, two hundred, five hundred, or more parishes or churches; yet he is the bridegroom of one church. The pope claims to be the bridegroom of all churches, both large and small, yet he is called the husband of one church. They are not bigamists or men with two wives, though they have all these brides at the same time. But he who marries a virgin who was betrothed to another is a bigamist. God will inflict gross, monstrous folly like this on us if we despise his word and want to do everything better than he commanded.

Indeed, they have an *acutius* in their *Decretum*, in which St. Augustine holds, against St. Jerome, that he who had a wife before baptism and also one after baptism had two wives. Dear asses, does it therefore follow that St. Augustine, even though he views such a man as the husband of two wives (something Scripture does not do), wishes to have him condemned and barred from serving God, as you do? And even though this should follow, do you not have a strong *noli meis* in dist. IX against it? How is it that you hold so fast to the *acutius* (though it is against Scripture) and pass so lightly over the *noli meis* and other chapters? This is, of course, your idea: you want to be lords of the church; whatever you say should be accepted as right. Marriage shall be right and a sacrament, if you will it so; on the oilier hand, marriage shall be an impurity, that is, a defiled sacrament that cannot serve God, if you will it so. Marriage shall bear children, and yet the wife shall remain a virgin or it is not a sacrament of Christ and the church, if you will it so. The bigamists are blameless and have a true marriage and sacrament, if you will it so; on the other hand, they are condemned and barred from serving God and have no sacrament of Christ and the church, if you will it so. Behold how the devil, who teaches you this nonsense, makes you reel and sway back and forth.

Why should I regard St. Augustine's statement as an article of faith if he himself does not wish to do so and if he himself does not even want to accept the sayings of his predecessors as articles of faith? Suppose that the dear fathers' opinion and teaching about a bigamist was such (as described)—what does it matter to us? It does not obligate us to hold and to teach that view. We must found our salvation on the words and works of man as little as we build our houses of hay and straw. But the canonists are such stupid asses and fools, with their idol in Rome, that they convert the words and deeds of the dear fathers into articles of faith against their will and without their consent. It should be proved by Scripture that such men may be called bigamists or trigamists; then their exclusion from the ministry of the church would be right and stand approved by St. Paul's instruction in I Timothy 3 [:2], "A bishop shall be the husband of one wife." But this frequently happened to the fathers—they sewed old patches on new cloth. This is the case here: no bigamist shall be a servant of the church; that is right and that is the new cloth. But that this or that man is really a bigamist, that is the old patch of their own opinion because Scripture does not say it. Scripture regards the man who has two wives living at the same time as a bigamist; and it is assumed that St. Paul had had a wife, Philippians 4 [:3], and that she died. So he too must have been a man with two wives, obliged to give up his apostolic office; for in I Corinthians 7 [:8] he counts himself among the widowed, and yet in I Corinthians 9 [:5] he, along with Barnabas, claims the right to be accompanied by a wife. Who will assure us that the poor fishermen, Peter, Andrew, and James, were married to virgins and not to widows, or that they did not have two wives in suecession?

These blockheads do not have the same idea of chastity that the fathers had, but would like to confuse the poor souls and jeopardize them, if only their stinking and filthy book is regarded as right and their "science" is not found to err or to have erred. Otherwise, they would indeed see what chastity is—since, with regard to other "opinions"[412] (and what is their best and foremost but a matter of mere opinion?), they can say nicely, "It is not held; but hold this." Why can they not do it here, especially since they do not hesitate to repudiate not only one father, but all of them, in "the eases to be decided,"[414] as their idol sputters and bellows? But they would like to rule the church, not with trustworthy wisdom, but with arbitrary opinions, and again confuse and perplex all the souls in the world, as they have done before. But just as they reject all the fathers and theologians in their petty canons, so do we, in turn, reject them in the church and in Scripture. They shall neither teach us Scripture nor rule in the church; they are not entitled to it, nor do they have the competence for it. But they shall attend to their trifling canons and squabbles over prebends—that is their holiness. They have cast us poor theologians, together with the fathers, from their books; for this we thank them most kindly. Now they propose to throw us out of the church and out of Scripture; and they themselves are not worthy to be in them. That is too much, and rips the bag wide open. And furthermore, we shall not put up with it.

I truly believe that in accordance with their wisdom no man could marry a virgin and, after her death, become a priest among them, for who can guarantee or vouch that he is actually getting a virgin? "The road runs past the door" (as they say). Now if he would find her not a virgin—and that is a chance he must take—he would, through no fault of his own, be a stinking bigamist. And if he wants to be certain that he can become a priest, he dare not marry a virgin either, for what assurance does he have that she is one? However, he may ravish virgins, widows, and wives, have many whores, commit all sorts of secret sins—he is still worthy of the priestly office. The sum and substance of it all is that the pope, the devil, and his church are averse to the estate of matrimony, as Daniel [11:37] says; therefore he wants it viewed as such a defilement that a married man cannot fill a priest's office. That is as much as to say that marriage is harlotry, sin, impure, and rejected by God. And even though they say, at the same time, that marriage is holy and a sacrament, that is hypocrisy and a lie, for if they would sincerely regard it as holy and a sacrament they would not forbid a priest to marry. But since they do prohibit it, it follows that they consider it impure and a sin—as they plainly say, "You must be clean, who bearest [the vessels of the lord]" or (if some really are that pious) they must be stupid Nestorians and Eutychians, affirming a premise and denying the conclusion. May this be the reception that we, for the time being, accord the papal ass and the asinine papists, as we return to our own people.

Therefore do not worry (as was said) about the papists' talk concerning the personal qualifications for an ecclesiastical office, for these asses do not understand St. Paul's words, nor do they know what St. Paul's language calls a sacrament. He says [Eph. 5:31–32] that Christ and the church are a sacrament, that is, Christ and the church are one body, as husband and wife are, and that this is a great mystery, to be apprehended by faith. It is not visible or tangible; therefore it is a sacrament, that is, something secret, a mystery, invisible, hidden. But since not only virginal but also widowed people entering matrimony are one body, every marriage is a figure or symbol of this great sacrament or mystery in Christ and the church. St. Paul speaks of neither virgins nor widows; he speaks of marriage, in which husband and wife are one body. Now wherever you find these offices or officers, you may be assured that the holy Christian people are there; for the church cannot be without these bishops, pastors, preachers, priests; and conversely, they cannot be without the church. Both must be together.

Sixth, the holy Christian people are externally recognized by prayer, public praise, and thanksgiving to God. Where you see and hear the Lord's Prayer prayed and taught; or psalms or other spiritual songs sung, in accordance with the word of God and the true faith; also the creed, the Ten Commandments, and the catechism used in public, you may rest assured that a holy Christian people of God are present. For prayer, too, is one of the precious holy possessions whereby everything is sanctified, as St. Paul says [I Tim. 4:5]. The psalms too are nothing but prayers in which we praise, thank, and glorify God. The creed and the Ten Commandments are also God's word and belong to the holy possession, whereby the Holy Spirit sanctifies the holy people of Christ. However, we are now speaking of prayers and songs which are intelligible and from which we can learn and by means of which we can mend our ways. The clamor of monks and nuns and priests is not prayer, nor is it praise to God; for they do not understand it, nor do they learn anything from it; they do it like a donkey, only for the sake of the belly and not at all in quest of any reform or sanctification or of the will of God.

Seventh, the holy Christian people are externally recognized by the holy possession of the sacred cross. They must endure every misfortune and persecution, all kinds of trials and evil from the devil, the world, and the flesh (as the Lord's Prayer indicates) by inward sadness, timidity, fear, outward poverty, contempt, illness, and weakness, in order to become like their head, Christ. And the only reason they must suffer is that they steadfastly adhere to Christ and God's word, enduring this for the sake of Christ, Matthew 5 [:11], "Blessed are you when men persecute you on my account." They must be pious, quiet, obedient, and prepared to serve the government and everybody with life and goods, doing no one any harm. No people on earth have to endure such bitter hate; they must be accounted worse than Jews, heathen, and Turks. In summary, they must be called heretics, knaves, and devils, the most pernicious people on earth, to the point where those who hang, drown, murder, torture, banish, and plague them to death are rendering God a service. No one has compassion on them; they are given myrrh and gall to drink when they thirst. And all of this is done not because they are adulterers, murderers, thieves, or rogues, but because they want to have none but Christ, and no other God. Wherever you see or hear this, you may know that the holy Christian church is there, as Christ says in Matthew 5 [:11–12], "Blessed are you when men revile you and utter all kinds of evil against you on my account. Rejoice and be glad, for your reward is great in heaven." This too is a holy possession whereby the Holy Spirit not only sanctifies his people, but also blesses them.

Meanwhile, pay no heed to the papists' holy possessions from dead saints, from the wood of the holy cross. For these are just as often bones taken from a carrion pit as bones of saints, and just as often wood taken from gallows as wood from the holy cross. There is nothing but fraud in this. The pope thus tricks people out of their money and alienates them from Christ. Even if it were a genuine holy possession, it would nonetheless not sanctify anyone. But when you are condemned, cursed, reviled, slandered, and plagued because of Christ, you are sanctified. It mortifies the old Adam and teaches him patience, humility, gentleness, praise and thanks, and good cheer in suffering. That is what it means to be sanctified by the Holy Spirit and to be renewed to a new life in Christ; in that way we learn to believe in God, to trust him, to love him, and to place our hope in him, as Romans 5 [:1–5] says, "Suffering produces hope," etc.

These are the true seven principal parts of the great holy possession whereby the Holy Spirit effects in us a daily sanctification and vivification in Christ, according to the first table of Moses. By this we obey it, albeit never as perfectly as Christ. But we constantly strive to attain the goal, under his redemption or remission of sin, until we too shall one day become perfectly holy and no longer stand in need of forgiveness. Everything is directed toward that goal. I would even call these seven parts the seven sacraments, but since that term has been misused by the papists and is used in a different sense in Scripture, I shall let them stand as the seven principal parts of Christian sanctification or the seven holy possessions of the church. (LW AE 41, 148-166)

[2] Luther's Small Catechism with Explanation, CPH: 1986, 147

[3] Barry, A.L., What About . . .*Fellowship in the Lord's Supper*

[4] Bonhoeffer, Dietrich, Life Together, Harper One, 22

[5] Bird, Chad, Personal notes on the Book of Genesis

[6] Harrison, Matthew C, Theology for Mercy, © 2004 The Lutheran Church—Missouri Synod

[7] Lutheran Service Book – Agenda, Rite of Holy Baptism, CPH: 2006, 6

[8] Ibid

[9] McCain, P. T. (Ed.). (2005). Concordia: The Lutheran Confessions (p. 419). St. Louis, MO: Concordia Publishing House.

[10] McCain, P. T. (Ed.). (2005). *Concordia: The Lutheran Confessions* (pp. 419–420). St. Louis, MO: Concordia Publishing House.

[11] Luther's Small Catechism with Explanation, CPH: 1986, 30-31

[12] McCain, P. T. (Ed.). (2005). *Concordia: The Lutheran Confessions* (p. 269). St. Louis, MO: Concordia Publishing House.

[13] Luther, M. (1999). *Luther's works, vol. 42: Devotional Writings I.* (J. J. Pelikan, H. C. Oswald, & H. T. Lehmann, Eds.) (Vol. 42, p. 122). Philadelphia: Fortress Press.

[14] Luther, M. (1999). *Luther's works, vol. 35: Word and Sacrament I.* (J. J. Pelikan, H. C. Oswald, & H. T. Lehmann, Eds.) (Vol. 35, p. 54).

Philadelphia: Fortress Press.
[15] Rev. Matthew C. Harrison, The Church Is a Mercy Place! © 2004 LCMS World Relief and Human Care
[16] Bray, G. (2000). *James, 1-2 Peter, 1-3 John, Jude*. Ancient Christian Commentary on Scripture NT 11 (223–224). Downers Grove, IL: InterVarsity Press.

[17] Eusebius of Caesaria. (1890). The Church History of Eusebius. In P. Schaff & H. Wace (Eds.), A. C. McGiffert (Trans.), *Eusebius: Church History, Life of Constantine the Great, and Oration in Praise of Constantine* (Vol. 1, p. 138). New York: Christian Literature Company.
[18] Eusebius of Caesaria. (1890). The Church History of Eusebius. In P. Schaff & H. Wace (Eds.), A. C. McGiffert (Trans.), *Eusebius: Church History, Life of Constantine the Great, and Oration in Praise of Constantine* (Vol. 1, p. 129). New York: Christian Literature Company.
[19] McCain, P. T. (Ed.). (2005). *Concordia: The Lutheran Confessions* (p. 341). St. Louis, MO: Concordia Publishing House.

[20] Korby, Kenneth, Cited online at http://www.goodshepherd.nb.ca/SelfExamination/SelfExamination.pdf
[21] White, Laurence, (1995) *LIFE WITH GOD: A Survey of Biblical Doctrine As Confessed in the Evangelical Lutheran Church* (pp. 217-222). Our Savior Lutheran Church – Houston, Texas

Made in the USA
Lexington, KY
16 November 2016